# THE
# RULES
## OF
# LIFE

*A personal code for living a
better, happier, and more
successful kind of life*

### Expanded Edition

## RICHARD TEMPLAR

Vice President, Publisher: Tim Moore
Associate Publisher and Director of Marketing: Amy Neidlinger
Acquisitions Editor: Megan Graue
Operations Manager: Gina Kanouse
Senior Marketing Manager: Julie Phifer
Publicity Manager: Laura Czaja
Assistant Marketing Manager: Megan Colvin
Cover Designer: Sandra Schroeder
Managing Editor: Kristy Hart
Senior Project Editor: Lori Lyons
Proofreader: Gill Editorial Services
Senior Compositor: Gloria Schurick
Manufacturing Buyer: Dan Uhrig

©2011 by Pearson Education, Inc.
Publishing as FT Press
Upper Saddle River, New Jersey 07458

Authorized adaptation from the original UK edition, entitled *The Rules of Life*,
Second Edition, by Richard Templar, published by Pearson Education Limited,
©Pearson Education 2010.

This U.S. adaptation is published by Pearson Education Inc,
©2010 by arrangement with Pearson Education Ltd, United Kingdom.

FT Press offers excellent discounts on this book when ordered in quantity for bulk
purchases or special sales. For more information, please contact U.S. Corporate
and Government Sales, 1-800-382-3419, corpsales@pearsontechgroup.com.
For sales outside the U.S., please contact International Sales at
international@pearson.com.

Company and product names mentioned herein are the trademarks or registered
trademarks of their respective owners.

Printed in the United States of America

Third Printing October 2012

ISBN-10: 0-13-248556-7
ISBN-13: 978-0-13-248556-2

Pearson Education LTD.
Pearson Education Australia PTY, Limited.
Pearson Education Singapore, Pte. Ltd.
Pearson Education North Asia, Ltd.
Pearson Education Canada, Ltd.
Pearson Educación de Mexico, S.A. de C.V.
Pearson Education—Japan
Pearson Education Malaysia, Pte. Ltd.

*Library of Congress Cataloging-in-Publication Data*
Templar, Richard, 1950-2006.
   The rules of life : a personal code for living a better, happier, more successful
life / Richard Templar. — Expanded ed.
      p. cm.
   Includes bibliographical references and index.
   ISBN 978-0-13-248556-2 (pbk. : alk. paper)
   1. Conduct of life. I. Title.
   BJ1581.2.T42 2011
   158.1—dc22
                                        2010038220

## Dedication

This book is dedicated to Miyamoto Musashi,
who taught me the strategy of simplicity,
and Jamie Greenwood, who taught me
economy of movement. I am indeed deeply
indebted to both of them
No Fear
No Surprise
No Hesitation
No Doubt

# Contents

# Introduction

For reasons that are too long and complicated to go into here, I had to live with my grandparents for a couple of years when I was very young. They, like many of their generation, were hard-working, contented sort of people. My grandfather had taken early retirement owing to an industrial accident (a truck-load of bricks fell on his foot) and my grandmother worked in a large department store in London. Having me dumped unexpectedly on her for a while obviously caused logistical problems. I was too young for school, and my grandfather wasn't to be trusted to look after me at home. (Men didn't look after children in those days...my, how things have changed.) Her solution was to tuck me under her wing—on some days physically as well as metaphorically, as she smuggled me past managers and supervisors—and we went to work together.

Now going to work with "Nan" was fun. I was expected to keep quiet and still for long periods and, as I didn't know any different, assumed this was normal. I found that by watching customers—often from my safe refuge under a huge desk—I could pass the time quite happily. Thus was born an immense appetite for people-watching.

My mother—later I went back to live with her—said it would never get me anywhere. I'm not so sure. You see, early in my career, observation of those around showed that there were a distinct set of behaviors that got people promoted. If there were two women of equal ability, for example, and one dressed, thought, and behaved as if she had already been promoted, she would be the one who got the next available job at that next level. Putting these behaviors into practice gave me a fast track up the career ladder. These "rules" formed the basis of my book Rules of Work, now a bestseller in its field.

Just as you can identify behaviors that make some people glide effortlessly onward and upward at work, so you can in life. Observing life in general, people very broadly seem to fall into two main camps: those who seem to have mastered the knack of successful living, and those who still find it all a bit of a struggle. And when I say successfully mastered it, I don't mean by amassing wealth or being at the top in some stressful career. No, I mean mastered it in the old-fashioned sense that my hard-working grandparents would have understood. People who are content, mostly happy on a day-to-day basis, and in general healthy and getting more out of life. Those who are still struggling tend to be not so happy on the whole, and the enjoyment of life just isn't what it should be.

So what's the secret? The answer comes down to a simple choice. We can all choose to do certain things every day of our lives. Some things we do will make us unhappy, and some things we choose to do will make us happier. By observing people, I have reasoned that if we follow a few basic "Rules of Life," we tend to get more done, shrug off adversity more easily, get more out of life, and spread a little happiness around us as we go. People who play by the Rules seem to bring their luck with them, light up a room when they enter, have more enthusiasm for life, and cope better.

So what follows are my Rules of Life. They aren't set in stone, and they aren't secret or difficult. And they are based entirely on my observations of happy and successful people. I have noticed that those who are happy are those who follow most of them. Those who seem miserable are the ones who don't follow them. And the successful ones often don't even realize this is what they are doing—they are natural Rules Players. Whereas the less instinctive ones often feel something is missing and spend their entire life looking for something—often themselves—that will miraculously give their life meaning or fill some empty void within them. But the answer lies much closer to home—simple changes in behavior are all that is required.

Can it really be that easy? No, of course not. To live by the Rules is never easy. If it was, we would all have stumbled on this a long time ago. It has to be hard to make it worthwhile. But, and this is the beauty of the Rules, they are all individually simple and attainable. You can aim high and go for them all or take one or two and start there. Me? No, I never get it all right, ever. I fall by the wayside as often as anyone else, but I do know what to do to get back up again. I know what I have to do to make my life make sense again.

By watching people, I came to realize that all of these Rules of Life are sensible. Personally I love the sort of advice that begins, "Go quietly…," but I'm not sure how I'm supposed to do that. However, a bit of advice such as, "Polish your shoes before you go out" makes more sense to me because that is something I can do and, more importantly, in which I can immediately see the logic. Incidentally, I still feel polished shoes make a better impression than scruffy ones.

You won't actually find shoe polishing here, nor will you find anything inspirational and New Age, which doesn't mean those things don't count. It's just that I feel it is better to have realistic things we can do rather than uplifting clichés that may well be true—time is a great healer, for example, and love does conquer all—but when you want things to do, clichés don't hit the button as far as I'm concerned.

What you will find here is good old-fashioned common sense. There is nothing here you don't already know. This book isn't a revelation; it's a reminder. It reminds you that the Rules of Life are universal, obvious, simple. Do them. They work.

But what about those who don't do them and still seem success-ful? Well, I'm sure we all know people who have acquired great wealth and who are ruthless, unpleasant, dictatorial, and sail morally pretty close to the wind. And if that is what you want, it is attainable. But I'm assuming you want to be able to sleep nights, live with yourself, and be a thoroughly nice person. And the beauty of all this is it is entirely down to personal choice. We all choose every day whether we are on the side of the angels or the beasts. The Rules of Life help you choose to be on the side of the angels, but it's not compulsory. Personally, when I go to sleep at night, I like to do a quick recap of my day and then, hopefully, I can say to myself, "Yep, good day, did OK," and feel proud of what I've achieved, rather than feeling regretful and dissatisfied with my actions and life. I like to go to sleep feeling I've made a difference, been kind to people rather than hurting them, spread a little happiness, had some fun and generally got nearer to 10 than 1 out of 10 for good behavior.

The Rules of Life aren't about making lots of money and being incredibly successful. (You might need to read The Rules of Work for that.) It is quite simply about how you feel inside, how you affect people around you, what sort of a friend, partner, and parent you are, what sort of impact you make on the world, and what sort of impression you leave in your wake.

I regard my books, sometimes, a little like children. I pat them on the head, wipe their nose, and send them out into the world. I like to know how they've been received. So if The Rules of Life makes a difference to you, or you have a Rule or two of your own that I've missed, I'm always interested in hearing from you. You can email me at *Richard.Templar@RichardTemplar.co.uk.*

*Richard Templar*

# Acknowledgments

I would like to thank all the readers who have emailed me over the years with comments on my books, and especially those who have contributed ideas to this new edition of The Rules of Life. In particular, may I thank:

Nicola Betts

Neil Duggan

Zakia Moulaoui

Daniel Nortey

Jalaj Soni

Elif Vatanoğlu

and Donna the pizza lady

# PART I

# RULES
# FOR YOU

I've divided the Rules of Life into four areas—you, your partner, your family and friends, and your social circle (including work and friends)—to represent the four unconscious circles we all draw around ourselves.

Let's begin with the most important of these, the Rules for ourselves—personal Rules, Rules for us. These are the Rules that will help get us out of bed in the mornings, face the world with a positive attitude, and navigate our way safely and successfully through our day, no matter what may arise. These are the Rules that will help reduce stress levels, give us the right kind of outlook, encourage us to set our own standards, and have goals to aim for.

I guess that for each and every one of us, these Rules will have to be adapted to take into account our upbringing, our age, and our situation. We all need to have personal standards to live up to. They will vary from person to person, but it is vitally important to have them. Without them we are adrift and unable to monitor how we are doing. With them we have a firm center, somewhere we can get back to, somewhere to touch base and recharge. They are our benchmark for personal progress.

But it's not all about standards; it's also about lightening up, having fun, and enjoying life.

# RULE 1

## Keep It Under Your Hat

You are about to become a Rules Player. You are about to embark on a life-changing adventure, possibly, if you choose to accept your mission. You are about to discover ways to become positive, happy, and successful in everything you do. So there's no need to say anything to anybody about it. Keep quiet. No one likes a smart arse. That's it. First Rule: *Keep It Under Your Hat.*

There may well be times when you do want to talk to other people about what you're doing because, quite naturally, you want to share it with somebody. Well, you can't and you don't. Let people find out for themselves with no clues from you. You may think this unfair, but it is actually fairer than you believe. If you tell them, they'll shy away. And quite rightly so—we all hate being preached at. It's a bit like when you give up smoking and suddenly find this new healthier way of living and you simply have to convert all your old smoking friends. Trouble is, they aren't ready to quit yet and you find they label you as smug or self-righteous or, even worse, an ex-smoker. And how we all hate those.

So the first Rule is, quite simply, don't preach, propagate, try to convert, shout from the rooftops, or even mention this.

You will get a warm glow from changing your attitude to life and having people ask what it is you have done, are doing, and you can say that it's nothing, merely a sunny day and you feel better/happier/livelier/whatever. There is no need to go into any detail because that's not really what people want to know. In fact, it's exactly the opposite of what they want to know. It's a bit like when someone asks how you are. What they want to really hear is just the one word, "Fine." Even if you are in the very pits of despair, that's all people want to hear because anything more requires commitment on their part. And for a casual "How are you?", that's most certainly not what they want. What they want is just "Fine." And then they can be about their business without any further involvement. If you don't say "Fine" but instead unburden yourself, they will back off pretty quickly.

And it's the same with being a Rules Player. No one really wants to know, so keep quiet. How do I know? Because when I wrote *The Rules of Work*, which turned a lot of people onto the ability to be successful in the workplace without having to resort to underhand means, I suggested the same thing and found it worked. Just get on with it, do it quietly, and go about your daily life happily and smugly without having to tell anyone anything.

> DON'T PREACH,
> PROPAGATE,
> OR EVEN MENTION THIS.

# You'll Get Older But Not Necessarily Wiser

There is an assumption that as we get older we will get wiser; not true, I'm afraid. But we can carry on being just as foolish, still making plenty of mistakes. It's just that we make new ones, different ones. We do learn from experience and may not make the same mistakes again, but there is a whole new pickle jar of fresh ones just lying in wait for us to trip up and fall into. The secret is to accept this and not to beat yourself up when you do make new ones. The Rule really is: Be kind to yourself when you do muck things up. Be forgiving, and accept that it's all part of that growing older but no wiser routine.

Looking back, we can always see the mistakes we made, but we fail to see the ones looming up. Wisdom isn't about not making mistakes, but about learning to escape afterward with our dignity and sanity intact.

When we are young, aging seems to be something that happens to, well, old people. But it does happen to us all, and we have no choice but to embrace it and roll with it. Whatever we do and however we are, the fact is we are going to get older. And this aging process does seem to speed up as we get older.

You can look at it this way—the older you get, the more areas you've covered to make mistakes in. There will always be new areas of experience where we have no guidelines and where we'll handle things badly, overreact, get it wrong. And the more flexible we are, the more adventurous, the more life-embracing, then the more new avenues there will be to explore—and make mistakes in, of course.

As long as we look back and see where we went wrong and resolve not to repeat such mistakes, there is little else we need to do. Remember that any Rules that apply to you also apply to everyone else around you. Others are all getting older, too. And not any wiser particularly. Once you accept this, you'll be more forgiving and kinder toward yourself and others.

Finally, yes, time does heal, and things do get better as you get older. After all, the more mistakes you've made, the less likely that you'll come up with new ones. The best thing is that if you get a lot of your mistakes over and done with early on in life, there will be less to learn the hard way later on. And that's what youth is all about: a chance to make all the mistakes you can and get them out of the way.

> WISDOM ISN'T ABOUT NOT MAKING MISTAKES BUT ABOUT LEARNING TO ESCAPE AFTERWARD WITH OUR DIGNITY AND SANITY INTACT.

# RULE 3

## Accept What Is Done Is Done

People make mistakes. Sometimes very serious ones. As often as not, the mistakes aren't deliberate or personal. Sometimes people just don't know what they are doing. This means that if, in the past, people have behaved badly toward you, it wasn't necessarily because they meant to be horrid, but because they were as naïve, as foolish, as human as the rest of us. They made mistakes in the way they brought you up or finished a relationship with you or whatever, not because they wanted to do it that way, but because they didn't know any different.

If you want to, you can let go of any feelings of resentment, of regret, of anger. You can accept that you are a fabulous human being because of all the bad things that have happened to you, not in spite of them. What is done is done, and you need to just get on with your life. Don't use the labels "good" and "bad." Yes, I know some of it is indeed bad, but it is how we let it affect us that is the real "bad." You could let all these things get you down, fizzle away internally like some emotional acid making you ill and resentful and stuck. But you will let them go, embrace them as character forming, and in general as positive rather then negative.

On paper I had a seriously dysfunctional childhood and for a while was resentful. I blamed my bizarre upbringing for all that was weak or dispirited or badly formed in me. It's so easy to do. But once I accepted that what was done was done, and that I could choose to forgive and get on with my life, things improved enormously. Not all of my siblings chose the same route, and they carried on building up the resentment until it overwhelmed them.

For me it was essential, if I wanted more out of my life, to embrace all the bad things as being an important part of me and to move on. In fact, I wanted them to fuel me into my future, to become positive to such an extent that I couldn't imagine being me without them. Now, if given the choice, I wouldn't change a thing. Yes, looking back, it was tough being the kid I was, living the life I did, but it has certainly helped make me, me.

I think the change occurred once I realized that even if I could get in front of me all the people who had "done me wrong," there would still be nothing they could do. I could shout at them, berate them, rant at them, but there would be nothing they could do to make amends or put things right. They, too, would have to accept that what's done is done. There is no going back, only forward. Make it a motto for life—keep moving forward.

WHAT IS DONE IS DONE,
AND YOU NEED TO
JUST GET ON
WITH YOUR LIFE.

# RULE 4

## Accept Yourself

If you accept that what's done is done, you are left with your-self exactly as you are. You can't go back and change anything, so you've got to work with what you've got. I'm not suggesting anything New Age here such as love yourself—that's far too ambitious. No, let's begin with simple accepting. Accepting is easy because it is exactly what it says—accepting. You don't have to improve or change or strive for perfection. Quite the opposite. Just accept.

That means accepting all the warts and emotional lumps and bumps, the bad parts, the weaknesses, and the rest of it. This doesn't mean we are happy with everything about ourselves, or that we are going to be lazy and lead a bad life. We are going to accept the way we are, initially, and then build on that. What we are not going to do is beat ourselves up because we don't like some parts. Yes, we can change lots, but that will come later. We're only up to Rule 4 here.

This has to be a Rule because there can be no choice here. We have to accept that we are the way we are—the result of every-thing that has happened. It all just is. You, like me, like all of us, are human. That means you're pretty complex. You come fully loaded with desires, anguish, sins, pettiness at times, mistakes, ill temper, rudeness, deviation, hesitation, and repe-tition. That's what makes a human being so wonderful:s the complexity. None of us can ever be perfect. We start with what we've got and who we are and then we can only make a choice, each day, to strive for some kind of better. And that's all people can ask of us—to make that choice. To be awake and aware, to be ready to do the right thing. And accept that some days you aren't going to make it. Some days you will,

# RULE 4

like all of us, fall far short. That's OK; don't beat yourself up. Pick yourself up and start again. Accept that you will fail from time to time and that you are human.

I know it can be hard at times, but once you have picked up the gauntlet of becoming a Rules Player, you're well on the path to improvement. Stop picking faults with yourself or giving yourself a hard time. Instead, accept that you are what you are. You're doing the best you can at this point in time, so give yourself a pat on the back and move on.

> YOU DON'T HAVE TO IMPROVE OR CHANGE OR STRIVE FOR PERFECTION. QUITE THE OPPOSITE. JUST ACCEPT.

# RULE 5

## Know What Counts and What Doesn't

Being here counts. Being kind and considerate counts. Getting through each day without seriously offending anyone or hurting anyone counts. Having the latest technology doesn't.

Sorry, I don't hate technology. In fact, I probably have pretty much all the latest gizmos. I just (a) don't overly rely too much on any of it and (b) see them all as useful tools rather than having any intrinsic meaning in themselves, in a status symbol or one-up kind of way.

Doing something useful with your life counts. Going shopping because you're bored doesn't. Yes, by all means go shopping, but see what you do as counting or not counting, being real or not being real, having real value or not, being of some benefit or not. This does not mean chucking it all up and going off to some fly-infested swamp to work with the locals and catch malaria—although that in itself would count, but you don't have to go to quite those extremes to make your life meaningful.

I guess the Rule means focusing on what is important to you in your life and making positive changes to ensure you feel happy with what you are dedicating your life to (see Rule 6). This doesn't mean long-term plans mapped out to the smallest detail. It means knowing, roughly, where you are going and what you are doing. Be awake rather than asleep. A fellow author, Tim Freke, calls it "lucid living"*—a perfect term for what we are talking about.

* Lucid Living by Tim Freke (Books for Burning, 2005).

# RULE 5

There are some things in this life that are important and a whole lot of things that aren't. It doesn't take too much discrimination to work out which are which. And there are a whole lot more things that don't count, aren't really important, to choose from. I'm not saying we can't have trivia in our lives—we can and it's fine. Just don't go mistaking the trivia for what is really important. Having time for loved ones and friends is important; watching the latest soap isn't. Repaying a debt is important; what brand of detergent you use isn't. Nurturing our children and teaching them real values is important; dressing them in designer fashion isn't. You get the idea. Think about what you do that counts—and do more of it.

THERE ARE SOME THINGS
IN THIS LIFE THAT ARE
IMPORTANT AND A WHOLE
LOT OF THINGS THAT
AREN'T.

# RULE 6

## Dedicate Your Life to Something

To know what counts and what doesn't, you have to know what you are dedicating your life to. There are, of course, no right or wrong answers to this one because it's a very personal choice—but it's really useful to have an answer, rather than not really knowing.

As an example, my own life has been driven by two things: (a) someone once told me that if my soul or spirit was the only thing I was likely to be taking with me when I went, then it ought to be the best thing I had; (b) my curious upbringing.

The first one isn't, for me at least, in any way religious. It just struck a chord with me, triggered something. Whatever it was I was taking with me, then perhaps I ought to do a bit of work on it. Make sure it really is the very best thing about me. That got me thinking. How on earth do you go about that? The answer still is that I haven't got a clue. I have explored and experimented, learned and made mistakes, been a seeker and a follower, read and observed, and wrestled with this great problem all my life. How do you go about improving your life on that level? I think the only conclusion I have come to is to live as decent a life as possible, to go through causing as little damage as possible, to treat everyone with whom you come into contact with respect and dignity. It's something to dedicate my life to, and it works for me.

And how can my curious upbringing cause me to focus on what I am dedicating my life to? Well, having had a "dysfunctional" upbringing and having chosen to let it motivate me rather than affect me, I am acutely aware that many people also need to discard that feeling of being badly affected by what has gone before. This is what I dedicate my life to. Yes, it might be crazy; I might be crazy. But at least I have something I can focus on, something (for me) that counts.

Now, none of this is big stuff, and by that I mean I don't go around with this emblazoned on my forehead—"Templar dedicates his life to ..." sort of thing. It's more that quietly, in my heart, I have something that I can devote my attention to. It's a yardstick by which I can measure (a) how I'm doing, (b) what I'm doing, and (c) where I'm going. You don't need to trumpet it. You don't need to tell anyone (see Rule 1). You don't even need to think it out in too much detail. A simple internal mission statement will do. Disney's mission, for example, is: "To make people happy." Decide what it is you are dedicating your life to. It makes the rest much easier.

IT'S A YARDSTICK
TO MEASURE
(A) HOW I'M DOING,
(B) WHAT I'M DOING, AND
(C) WHERE I'M GOING.

# RULE 7

# Be Flexible in Your Thinking

Once your thinking gets crystallized, rigid, and formed, you've lost the battle. Once you think you have all the answers, you might as well hang up your boots. Once you get set in your ways, you're already part of history.

To get the most out of life, you have to keep all your options open, keep your thinking and life flexible. You have to be ready to roll as the storm breaks—and, by golly, it always breaks when you least expect it. The instant you are established in a set pattern, you set yourself up for being knocked off-course. You might need to examine your thinking pretty closely to understand what I mean. Flexible thinking is a bit like mental martial arts—being ready to duck and weave, dodge and flow. Try to see life not as the enemy, but as a friendly sparring partner. If you're flexible, you'll have fun. If you stand your ground, you're likely to get knocked about a bit.

We all have set patterns in life. We like to label ourselves as this or that and are quite proud of our opinions and beliefs. We all like to read a set paper, watch the same sorts of TV shows or movies, go to the same sort of shops every time, eat the sort of food that suits us, wear the same type of clothes. And all this is fine. But if we cut ourselves off from all other possibilities, we become boring, rigid, hardened—and thus likely to get knocked about a bit.

You have to see life as a series of adventures. Each adventure is a chance to have fun, learn something, explore the world, expand your circle of experience and friends, and broaden your horizons. Shutting down to adventure means exactly that—you are shut down.

The second you are offered an opportunity to have an adventure, to change your thinking, to step outside of yourself, go for it and see what happens. If this thought scares you, remember that you can always go back into your shell the second it's over, if you want to.

But even saying yes to every opportunity isn't set in stone as a rule, because that would be inflexible. The really flexible thinkers know when to say "no" as well as when to say "yes."

If you want to know how flexible your thinking is, here are a couple of tests. Are the books by the side of your bed the same sorts of books you've always read? Have you found yourself saying anything like, "I don't know any people like that" or "I don't go to those kind of places"? If so, then perhaps it's time to broaden your mind and take the shackles off your thinking.

> TRY TO SEE LIFE NOT AS
> THE ENEMY, BUT AS A
> FRIENDLY SPARRING
> PARTNER.

# RULE 8

## Take an Interest in the Outside World

You may be wondering why this Rule is here and not in with the ones in the section about the world. Well, this one is about you. Taking an interest in the outside world is about developing you, rather than for the world's benefit. I'm not suggesting you have to watch the news constantly, but by reading, listening, and talking, we keep abreast of what is happening. Successful Rules Players don't get bogged down by the minutiae of their own lives; they don't live in a tiny bubble. Make it your mission to know what's going on in the world—in current events, music, fashion, science, movies, food, transport, even TV. Successful Rules Players are able to hold a conversation on pretty much everything and anything because they are interested in what's going on. You don't necessarily have to own the latest everything, but you should have a rough idea of what is changing, what's new, and what's happening, both in your community and on the other side of the world.

And the benefits? Well, for starters it makes you more interesting as a person, and it keeps you young. I met an elderly woman in the post office the other day who was going on about PIN numbers, "PIN numbers, PIN numbers—what do I want with PIN numbers at my age?" The short answer is that of course she needs them; she can't get her pension money without them. But it's more than that. It is terribly easy to sink into the, "I've never done this before, so I don't need to do it now" mentality. If we do this, we stand a good chance of really missing out.

The happiest, most well-balanced, most successful people in life are those who are part of something. Part of the world, not cut off from it. And the most interesting, stimulating people to

be around are those who take a great interest in what's happening around them. Listening to the radio the other
morning, the head of the American prison service was being
interviewed and was talking about penal reform, a subject I
have no interest in personally. (I don't know anyone inside.)
You could argue that I didn't need to know about the
American prison service any more than the old woman needed
to know about PIN numbers, but I felt more stimulated and
alive and interested for it. And that can't be bad.

> TAKING AN INTEREST IN
> THE OUTSIDE WORLD IS
> ABOUT DEVELOPING YOU,
> RATHER THAN FOR THE
> WORLD'S BENEFIT.

# RULE 9

# Be on the Side of the Angels, Not the Beasts

Every single day of our lives we are faced with an immense number of choices. And each and every one of them usually boils down to a simple choice between being on the side of the angels or the beasts. Which are you going to pick? Or did you not even realize what was going on? Let me explain. Every action we take has an effect on our family, people around us, society, the world in general. And that effect can be positive or detrimental—it's usually our choice. And sometimes it is a difficult choice. We get torn between what we want and what is good for others—personal satisfaction or magnanimity.

Look, no one said this was going to be easy. And making the decision to be on the side of the angels is often a tough call. But if we want to succeed in this life—and I measure success by how close we get to generating that self-satisfaction/happiness/contentment—then we have to consciously do this. This can be what we dedicate our lives to—angels and not beasts.

If you want to know if you have already made the choice, just do a quick check of how you feel and how you react if someone cuts in front of you in a line of traffic in the rush hour. Or when you're in a big hurry and someone stops to ask you for directions. Or if you have teenage children and one of them gets into trouble with the police. Or when you lend a friend money and he fails to pay it back. Or if your boss calls you a fool in front of the rest of your colleagues. Or your neighbor's trees start to encroach on your property. Or you hit your thumb with the hammer. Or, or, or. As I said, it is a choice we have to make every day, lots of times. And it has to become a conscious choice to be effective.

Now, the problem is that no one is going to tell you exactly what constitutes an angel or a beast. Here you are going to have to set your own parameters. But come on, it can't be that difficult. I think an awful lot of it is self-evident. Does it hurt or hinder? Are you part of the problem or the solution? Will things get better or worse if you do certain things? You have to make this choice for yourself alone.

It is your interpretation of what is an angel or beast that counts. There is no point in telling anyone else that they are on the side of the beasts, as they may have a totally different definition. What other people do is their choice, and they won't thank you for telling them otherwise. You can, of course, watch, as an impassive, objective observer and think to yourself: "I wouldn't have done it like that." Or "I think they just chose to be an angel." Or even, "Gosh, how beastly." But you don't have to say anything.

> ## WE GET TORN BETWEEN WHAT WE WANT AND WHAT IS GOOD FOR OTHERS.

# Only Dead Fish Swim with the Stream

Life is difficult. And the Rule is to thank God* it is so. If it was all fluffy and easy, we wouldn't be tested, tried, forged in the fire of life. We wouldn't grow or learn or change or have a chance to rise above ourselves. If life were a series of lovely days, we'd soon get bored. If there was no rain, then there wouldn't be any feeling of great joy when it finally stopped and we could go to the beach. If it was all easy we couldn't get stronger.

So, be thankful it is a struggle some of the time, and recognize that only dead fish swim with the stream. For the rest of us, there will be times when it's an uphill, upstream struggle. We will have to battle waterfalls, dams, and raging torrents. But we have no choice. We have to keep swimming or get swept away. And each flick of our tail, each surge of our fins, makes us stronger and fitter, leaner and happier.

There is a statistic that suggests that for a lot of men, retirement is a really bad idea. Lots of them die within a relatively short time of handing in their briefcase.** They have ceased to swim against the current and get swept away. Keep swimming, little fish, keep swimming.

Try to see each setback as a chance to improve. Trials make you stronger, not weaker. You only get burdened with as much as you can carry—although I do appreciate that at times it may seem as if it's a whole lot more. And, of course, the struggles don't come to an end, but there are lulls in-between times—backwaters where we can rest for a while and enjoy

* Or whoever or whatever you choose to so thank. Don't write in.
** I don't know if this affects women just as adversely. You may write in.

the moment before the next obstacle gets thrown our way. And that's what life is, what it is meant to be: a series of struggles and lulls. And whatever situation you're in now, it's going to change. So what are you in? Lull or struggle? Rain or going to the beach? Learning or enjoying? Dead fish or healthy salmon?

AND THAT'S WHAT LIFE IS,
WHAT IT IS MEANT TO BE:
A SERIES OF STRUGGLES
AND LULLS.

# RULE 11

# Be the Last to Raise Your Voice

For me this is a really hard one. I do love to have a good shout. I came from a big, robust family where shouting was a way of life and the only way to get yourself heard, get any attention, or make a point. Dysfunctional? Yes. Noisy? Yes. Helpful? Probably not.

One of my sons has inherited the shouting gene, and he is very good at it. The temptation is to join in. Luckily, this Rule is be the last to raise your voice, so I do have a get-out clause. If he shouts first, I'm allowed to shout back. But I do try really hard not to. For me, shouting in any form is a bad thing, a sign that I have lost control, lost the argument. The son of a vicar once saw his father's sermon notes and in the margin he had pencilled, "Shout here, argument weak." I think this just about sums it all up.

But I have shouted at various times and, invariably, I regret each and every occasion. I know I've regretted the time I was very shouty in a well-known high street electrical chain over a damaged video player. At that time I did get my own way, but the reality is that it was a bad thing and deep down I'm quite ashamed of myself.

So what do you do if you, too, have inherited the shouty gene like I have? I find that I have to walk away to stop the inevitable decline into shouting in a challenging situation. That's a tough one, especially if you know you're right. There are so many things that make us shout, so many situations where we feel that a judicious loss of temper will get us our own way. But we are dealing with real live human beings who have their own feelings, and shouting is not justified—even if they start it first.

There are two situations where people lose their temper—justified and manipulative. The first is where you run over their foot with your car and refuse to apologize or acknowledge you have done anything wrong. In this situation, they are allowed to shout. The second situation is where people use anger to get their own way—a sort of emotional blackmail. You are allowed to ignore them or to be assertive to control the situation. You are not allowed to shout back.

I know, I know, there are all sorts of situations where shouting seems appropriate—the dog is stealing the Sunday dinner; the kids won't tidy their room; your computer has crashed again and the repair department won't fix it quickly enough; the local deliquents are adorning your fence, again; after going through the umpteen options over and over again, you fail to get through to the receptionist after holding for 20 minutes; the clerk put up the closed sign just as you get to the counter; someone is clearly being stupid and deliberately choosing to misunderstand you.

And on and on and on. But if you take this Rule as a simple "I don't do shouting," it becomes an easy benchmark to stick to. You become known as someone who is incredibly calm no matter what is happening. Calm people are trusted. Calm people are relied on. Calm people are looked up to and given responsibility. Calm people last longer.

> SHOUT HERE,
> ARGUMENT WEAK.

# RULE 12

## Be Your Own Adviser

Deep down within all of us is a fount of wisdom. This is called intuition. Listening to your intuition is a slow-learned process. It starts by recognizing that tiny inner voice or feeling that will tell you when you've done something you shouldn't have. It's an incredibly still, quiet voice and needs silence and concentration to hear it properly to begin with.

You might like to call it your conscience if you like, but deep down you know when you've done something bad. You know when you've got to apologize, make amends, put things right. You know. And I know you know. I know because we all know. There's no getting away from it.

Once you start listening to that inner voice or feeling the feeling, you'll find it can help. It will become more than a mindless parrot perched on your shoulder, chanting, "You messed up again" after the event. The key is when you hear your intuition telling you whether something is the right thing to do or not—before you do it.

Try running stuff past your inner you *before* doing things and see what reaction you get. Once you get used to this, you'll find it easier. Imagine, in any situation, that you have a small child standing at your side and you have to explain things to them. Imagine that she asks questions—"Why are you doing that? What's right and wrong? Should we do this?"—and you have to answer. Only in this situation, you ask the questions and you answer yourself. And you'll find you already know everything there is to know and everything you'll ever need to know.

Listen, and it's all there. If you are going to trust any adviser, who will it be? It makes sense for it to be you because you have all the facts, all the experience, all the knowledge at your fingertips. No one else has. No one can get inside you and see exactly what's going on.

Quick point of clarification here. When I say listen, I don't mean listen to what goes on in your head. Now that really is where madness lies. No, I mean a stiller, quieter voice. For some it's more a feeling than a voice—what we sometimes call gut instinct. And even if it is a voice, a lot of the time it doesn't speak at all—unlike our mind, which babbles on incessantly—and if it does, you can miss it in the torrent of words that our mind produces.

This isn't about predicting what's going to happen. You won't discover which horse will win the Kentucky Derby or who'll score in the Cup Final. No, this is the important stuff: what we're about to do, big decisions we have to make, why we are behaving in the way we are. You already know the answer, if you ask yourself.

YOU KNOW.
AND I KNOW YOU KNOW.
I KNOW BECAUSE
WE ALL KNOW.

# RULE 13

# No Fear, No Surprise,
# No Hesitation, No Doubt

Where does this come from? It's from a seventeenth-century samurai warrior. This was his four-point key to successful living—and swordsmanship.

## No Fear

There should be nothing in this life that you are afraid of. If there is, you might need to do some work on overcoming that fear. Here I have to confess to a certain fear of heights. I avoid high places if I can. Recently, owing to leaky gutters, I had to crawl out on our roof—three floors up with a very long drop on one side. I gritted my teeth and kept repeating, "No fear, no fear, no fear," until the job was done. Oh yes, and of course I didn't look down. Whatever your fear, face it head on and defeat it.

## No Surprise

Life seems to be full of surprises, doesn't it? You're going along swimmingly and suddenly something huge rears up ahead of you. But if you look carefully, there were clues all along the way that it was going to happen. No surprise there then. Whatever your situation now, it is going to change. No surprises there. So why does life seem to surprise us then? Because we are asleep half the time. Wake up, and nothing can sneak up on you.

## No Hesitation

Weigh the odds and then just get on with it. If you hang back, the opportunity will have passed. If you spend too long thinking, you'll never make a move. Once we have looked at the options, we make a choice and then go for it. That's the secret. No hesitation means not waiting around for other people to help out or make up our minds for us. No hesitation means if there is a certain inevitability about a situation, then just throw yourself in head first and enjoy the ride. If there is nothing to be done, then waiting doesn't help.

## No Doubt

Once you have made your mind up about something, don't go over it again and again. Stop thinking and enjoy—relax and let go. Stop worrying. Tomorrow will come along as certainly as it can. There is no doubt about life. It just is. Be confident. Be committed. Be sure of yourself. Once you have committed yourself to a set course, a path, a plan, then follow it through. Have no doubt it was the right thing to do and no doubt that you will succeed. Get on with it and trust your judgment completely.

# RULE 14

# I Wish I'd Done That—and I Will

Regrets, I've had a few…. You might be expecting me to say there's no room for regrets or "if onlys." As it happens, they can be very useful—if you choose to use them to make a difference going forward.

There are three types of "I wish I'd done that" scenarios. The first is when you genuinely feel you didn't capitalize on an opportunity or that you missed out on something. The second is when you see somebody who's done something great and you wish it had been you. The final type is not you, but the others—the people who hang around with a sort of permanent "I could have been a contender" mentality. If only I'd had the chances, the lucky breaks, the opportunities. For this last group, the bad news is that even if Lady Luck had come up and bitten them on the behind, they'd still have missed it.

When it comes to looking at what others have achieved, this world is divided into those who look at others enviously and those who look at others as a motivational tool. If you find yourself saying, "I wish I had done that/thought that/been there/seen that/experienced that/met them/understood that," then you need to learn to follow it up with a "And now, I will…."

In many cases the thing you wished you'd done might not be out of the question—even if it's not exactly as you would have done it previously. For example, if you're thinking "I wish I'd taken a year off before college and traveled to China like so and so did," then you're clearly not going to be able to reverse time. But could you get a sabbatical for six months and go now? Could you take a longer-than-usual vacation and go (with family if necessary)? Or how about making firm plans that when you retire you'll put this at the top of your "to do" list?

Obviously, if the regret is that you didn't win an Olympic 400m gold medal because you gave up athletics at 14, it's not going to happen if you're now 34. What you can do is resolve not to let any more opportunities pass you by. So you can choose to book those scuba diving lessons and, in doing so, ensure that you won't be saying, "I wish I'd learned to dive" in another 20 years' time.

THE WORLD IS DIVIDED INTO THOSE WHO LOOK AT OTHERS ENVIOUSLY AND THOSE WHO LOOK AT OTHERS AS A MOTIVATIONAL TOOL.

# It's OK to Give Up

You know how you sometimes hear stories about people who have failed their driving test 35 times? Much as you admire their persistence, don't you sometimes wonder why they don't just give up? These are clearly people who just aren't cut out to drive big, heavy, dangerous lumps of machinery around streets full of children and old people and dogs and lamp posts. Even if they do finally pass, there's a feeling that it's probably a fluke, and you probably still wouldn't want to be a passenger on their next trip.

Actually, if these people held their hands up (as some do) and said, "You know what? This isn't me. I'm going to get a bicycle and a bus season ticket," I would applaud their ability to see what was staring them in the face. I wouldn't call them quitters or criticize their lack of determination or drive.* They'd simply be getting the message loud and clear and having the good sense not to ignore it.

Sometimes we head off down the wrong path in life, often with the best motives. Maybe there's no knowing it's the wrong path until we try it. There's no shame in admitting it once we realize it's not getting us where we want to be. When you realize this college course isn't right for you, or that you don't have what it takes to do this job well, or that your move to a new city isn't working out, or that the hours you put into being on the local council put too much strain on your family, it takes guts to say so. That's not quitting. That's courage.

* Sorry, couldn't resist that one.

Quitting is when you give up because you don't want to put in the effort, you can't be bothered, you don't like hard work, you're scared of failure. We Rules players don't quit. We harden our resolve, and we get on with the job without complaint.

However, good Rules players know when they're beat. If the world is telling you that you took a wrong turn, you can admit it honestly and put yourself on a different track. No one can be brilliant at everything, and sometimes you have to try things to find out whether you can do them. And maybe you can't.

A few years ago, a leading UK government official resigned from her post, famously saying that she was simply "not up to the job." Now, I'd never really rated her up to that point, but she rose hugely in my estimation—and that of many others—for that admission. That took guts. Maybe she wasn't great at leading a government department, but she was certainly in a different league from most politicians when it came to honesty, courage, and self-knowledge. She's an outstanding example of the fact that if you give up in the right way at the right time, you're showing strength of character, not weakness.

GOOD RULES PLAYERS
KNOW WHEN THEY'RE
BEAT.

# Count to Ten—or Recite "Baa Baa Black Sheep"

Every now and then someone or something is really going to get your goat. But you're a Rules Player now, and you're not going to lose your temper any more. How, exactly? The answer is in fact one of those old pearls of wisdom. You get in the habit of counting to ten under your breath while you hope and pray that the feeling of impending rage will subside. It invariably does for me and gives me those vital seconds to regain my composure and remember where I am and who I am. Once I have collected my wits and calmed down, I can find an appropriate response.

But that counting to ten is essential. "Old hat," I hear you say. Yep, but it works. You don't like it? Then you are most welcome to find something else to recite under your breath. A poem perhaps, but it has to be a short one. That's why I suggested "Baa Baa Black Sheep."

Someone asks you a question and you're not sure of the answer. Take ten before you answer. This person will think you are incredibly wise and thoughtful. (Don't tell him if you are actually reciting "Baa Baa Black Sheep.") It's a variant on "engage brain before opening mouth," too—that extended pause can save endless trouble.

If you find yourself in a confrontational situation, taking a quiet ten can help enormously. I was once in a rough part of a town but very hungry so I ventured into a fish and chip shop. As I was being served, the "rough diamond" behind me whispered that I should be very careful when I left the shop. I asked why, and he said that I would be relieved of my food when I got outside by the local boys who were sitting on a brick wall. "Saves waiting in the queue," he confided.

I left the shop with trepidation—no wait, it was actually fear. But I buttoned up my coat, took a deep breath, and stood there looking at the youths. I counted to ten slowly while we all eyed each other, and then I walked toward them very purposefully. As I got to them, still counting, they turned away and I was left alone. God, those fish and chips tasted wonderful!

ONCE I HAVE COLLECTED
MY WITS AND
CALMED DOWN,
I CAN FIND AN
APPROPRIATE RESPONSE.

# RULE 17

## Change What You Can Change; Let Go of the Rest

Time is short. This is another of those facts you can't escape; it's a given. If time is short, then it makes sense not to go wasting any of it, not a single lovely drop of it. It's my observation that the successful people in this life are the ones who wring every last ounce of satisfaction and energy out of life. They do that by practising this simple Rule. They pay attention to what, in their life, they have some control over and they simply, economically (time-wise), let go of the rest.

If someone asks you directly for help, then that's something you can do—or not as you choose. If the whole world asks you for help, then there is very little you can do. Beating yourself up over it is counterproductive and such a waste of time. Now, I'm not saying to stop caring about things or to walk away from those in need. In fact, quite the opposite in many ways, but there are areas in which you can make a personal difference and other areas where you'll never even make a dent.

If you waste time struggling to change stuff that is obviously never going to be changed, then life will whiz past and you'll miss it. If, on the other hand, you dedicate yourself personally to things you can change, areas where you can make a difference, then life becomes richer and more fulfilled. And the more rich it is, curiously, the more time you seem to have.

Obviously, if lots of us get together, we can change pretty well anything, but this is a Rule for You—these are your personal set—and thus this is about what *you* can change.

If you have the ear of a president, you might be able to shape policy that affects the entire nation. If you have the ear of the

Pope, you might have a hand in shaping the next Papal Bull. If you have the ear of a general, you might avert a war. If you have the ear of an editor, you might get your name in print. If you have the ear of the head waiter, you might get the best table. And so on and so on. So whose ear have you got? What influence do you have, and what change can you effect by using that influence?

Often the only ear we have is our own. The only definite influence we have is over ourselves. The only thing we can really, really change is exactly that—ourselves. Wonderful. What an opportunity to do some good. What a chance to make a real contribution. Begin with ourselves and let it spread outward. This way we don't have to waste time preaching to those who won't listen. We don't have to waste effort or energy or resources on things over which we have no control and no certainty of any success. By changing ourselves, though, we can be assured of a result.

DEDICATE YOURSELF
PERSONALLY TO THINGS
YOU CAN CHANGE, AREAS
WHERE YOU CAN MAKE A
DIFFERENCE.

# RULE 18

## Aim to Be the Very Best at Everything You Do— Not Second Best

Wow. What a tall order. This is a seriously difficult thing to aim for—and deliberately so. If you go to work, then do your job as well as is humanly possible. If you are a parent, be the very best parent possible. If you are a gardener, be the very best gardener you can be. Because if you aren't, then what are you aiming for? And why? If you set out to do something, anything, and you are deliberately aiming for second best, how sad is that? This Rule is really simple, really easy. Let's take parenting, for example. What is the very best way of parenting possible? There are, of course, no right or wrong answers here—it's entirely a subjective assessment. What do you think the very best parenting means? Good. Now are you going to aim for less than that? Of course not.

And the same is true for everything you do. You aim to be the very best that you think is possible. Once you become the judge, the panel of experts, it is very easy to live up to those expectations because they are entirely yours. No one else can say whether you have failed or succeeded. No one else can set the criteria for what you are about to embark on.

Look, maybe this is a trick. If only you can judge whether you have succeeded, then obviously you are going to score 10 out of 10 every time. Aren't you? Probably not. It is amazing how tough we are on ourselves when no one is looking. If we are only cheating ourselves, then we realize there simply isn't any point to it.

The most marvelous thing about setting your own standards is that no one else can judge; others can't get their sticky little fingers on what, for you, is right or wrong, good or bad. How liberating is that? Infinitely. Having established that you'll aim for the very best and you've set the standards of what that is, all you have to do is periodically check back to that standard to see how you are doing.

None of this has to be incredibly detailed. For instance, your view of being the best parent could be as simple as "I'll always be there for them." You don't have to provide details, even if it is just for yourself, of how many times a day you'll tell them you love them, or whether you make sure they wear clean socks every day. No, your aim is simply "To be there for them, always," and that is your very, very best. Now, if you fail, it is only because you weren't there for them. Failing is fine. Aiming for second best isn't.

All you have to do is consciously think about what you are doing and then aim for that, the best. The secret is to be aware of what you are doing and have some sort of benchmark where you, and only you, monitor your performance. Make your goals, your aims, simple and obviously attainable. Make sure you know what is, for you, best and second best.

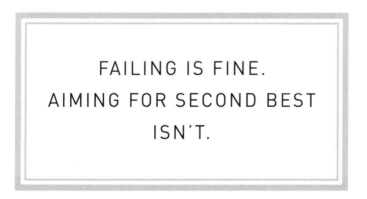

FAILING IS FINE.
AIMING FOR SECOND BEST
ISN'T.

# RULE 19

# Don't Expect to Be Perfect

OK, so you're aiming to be the very best at everything. But what if you fail? So long as you tried, that's all right. Who have you ever met who never failed at anything, however small? You're allowed to be human, you know. In fact, you're actively encouraged to be human. Don't try to set yourself above everyone else—the rest of us fail from time to time.

If you're not a perfectionist in any way—sloppy, haphazard, unorganized, messy, and with a "so what" attitude, please skip this section. But I hardly know anyone like that. I have a friend who is a silversmith. His house is a mess, his personal life is all over the place, but every piece of jewelry he turns out has to be exactly right. Most of us have some perfectionist tendencies.

My jeweler friend is quite right that every piece of work has to be perfect (certainly at his prices). If any piece is faulty, he shouldn't sell it. But that doesn't mean that he should beat himself up for having failed. He can just recognize that not everything works out and get to work on the next piece.

I can't stand people who seem perfect. They make me feel inadequate. And that's not a nice way to go through life, is it? Going around making other people feel inadequate. So let's have none of it. Let's all aim to be the best but acknowledge that it won't always happen. Just like gemstones, it's the flaws, the weaknesses, the imperfections that lend character. A flaw in a gemstone may detract from its value (though not always), but it also proves that it's genuine.

You are the sum total of everything that has happened in your life—the successes and the failures, the achievements and the mistakes. If you were to take any of the imperfect bits out of that equation, you wouldn't be you.

This Rule really does belong with the last one because I'm not saying that you can be uncommitted and half-hearted about everything you do because you don't need to be perfect. And as a Rules Player, I'm sure you wouldn't take it that way. The point is that so long as you're aiming for the best, you shouldn't beat yourself up when you don't always make it. Not only that, but you should celebrate your flaws and imperfections as an important and necessary part of you. This is an attitude that will make you a lot more fun to be around, I can tell you.

CELEBRATE YOUR FLAWS
AND IMPERFECTIONS AS
AN IMPORTANT AND
NECESSARY PART OF YOU.

# Don't Be Afraid to Dream

This may seem incredibly obvious, incredibly easy, but you would be surprised how many people seriously limit their dreams. They're your dreams, for heaven's sake. There should be no limit to them. Plans have to be realistic; dreams don't.

I worked in the casino business for many years and was always intrigued that "punters" (what we should really call "customers") could never see it; that they would always lose because they wouldn't limit their losses but would always limit their winnings. Don't ask me why. I guess addicted gamblers are seriously not well. They'd go in with the right attitude—"I'll just lose this $100 and then pack it in." Result: They'd lose the $100 and cash a check to chase it. Then another to chase the lost check. And another.

I'm not advocating gambling, by the way—not now, not ever. It's really not a good idea, believe me. The point is that people limit their dreams the way they limit their winnings. And yet dreams are at worst harmless. Don't limit them! You are allowed to dream as high, as wide, as big, as extravagant, as impossible, as wacky, as silly, as bizarre, as unrealistically non-sensical as you want.

You are allowed to wish for anything you want as well. Look, wishes and dreams are private affairs. There are no wish police, no dream doctors who are on the rampage looking out for unrealistic demands. It is a private thing between you and ... that's it. Between you and absolutely no one else at all.

The only note of caution here—and I do speak from personal experience—is to be very careful of what you do wish for, what you dream of, because it might just come true. And where would you be then?

A lot of people think their dreams have to be realistic to be worth dreaming about. But that's a plan, and that is something quite different. I have plans, and I take logical steps to make them come to fruition. Dreams are allowed to be so improbable that they are never likely to come true. And don't go thinking you'll never achieve anything by sitting around daydreaming all day. Some of the most successful people have also been those who have dared to dream the most. It isn't a coincidence.

PLANS HAVE TO BE
REALISTIC;
DREAMS DON'T.

# If You're Going to Jump Off a Bridge, Make Sure You Know How Deep the Water Is

Me, I've always been a risk-taker. Too much of a risk-taker, some might say. In the long term, I haven't regretted the things I've done in life because they've made me who I am, and anyway you never know where the alternative would have gotten you. In the short term, however, I have often caught myself thinking, "You idiot! Why didn't you see that coming?"

The answer, of course, is because I didn't check how deep the water was before I jumped. There was the time I gave up a very good, steady job to become a writer. Didn't think about how long it would take to make any money as a writer.* Didn't plan out whether my savings would last. Didn't calculate what the mortgage, bills, weekly shopping, car, pet food, and all the rest would cost me with a new lifestyle. Well, eventually I started to make a living from my writing, but there were some pretty sticky years first, I can tell you.

I've always been terrified of ending up like those people I know who never take risks and who never go anywhere, change, grow, do anything, realize their dreams. I've seen it too often, and I don't want my name added to the list, thank you. But over the years, I've noticed that the people who are really happy are the ones who take risks, sure, but they look ahead first. Not looking for excuses to stay on the shore, but looking to see how deep the water is. As I've learned (shamefully slowly) to copy their example, I've found it makes me happier, too. I get what I want, and without paying as heavily for it as I often used to.

* The answer, if you're wondering, is several years.

I've been gullible in the past. Friends have said, "Come in, the water's lovely! Join us in this business venture/vacation/game." And I've just jumped in without looking. Funnily enough, sometimes it's turned out that the water is actually cold, murky, muddy, clammy. And invariably wet. Ugh! I've also had friends ask me to support them in ways that I haven't thought through. There's an instinct to help your friends when they're in trouble, but sometimes a loan that isn't repaid is more than you can afford. Or putting in time to listen to their troubles invades so much of your life that your family suffers.

So whether you're jumping off that bridge with a friend or on your own, just check the depth first. The water may indeed be lovely, but sometimes it's better to stand on a bank and dip a toe in, or paddle about a bit, so you have a better idea what it is you're jumping in to.

> SOMETIMES IT'S BETTER
> TO STAND ON A BANK AND
> DIP A TOE IN,
> OR PADDLE ABOUT A BIT.

# RULE 22

## Don't Dwell on the Past

Whatever the past was, it's gone. There is nothing you can do to change anything that has gone before, and so you must turn your attention to the here and now. It is hard to resist the allure of dwelling on what has gone before. But if you want to be successful in your life, you have to turn your attention to what is happening for you right now. You might be tempted to dwell on the past because it was awful or because it was wonderful. Either way, you have to leave it behind because the only way to live is in the present.

If you're revisiting the past because of regrets, then you need to be clear that you can't go back and undo what you've done. If you hang on to guilt, you're only damaging yourself. We've all made bad decisions that have adversely affected people around us that we professed to love but whom we treated disgracefully. There isn't anything you can do to wipe the slate clean. What you can do is to resolve not to make such bad decisions again. That's all anyone can ask of us—that we acknowledge where we messed up and are trying our hardest not to repeat the pattern.

If the past was better for you and you hanker after your glory days, then learn to appreciate the memories but also move on and put your efforts into finding a different kind of good time right now. If it truly was better back then (take off those rose-tinted spectacles for a minute), maybe you can analyze exactly why—money, power, health, vitality, fun, youth. Then move on to find other avenues to explore. We all have to leave good stuff behind and find new challenges, new areas to inspire us.

Every day that we wake up is a fresh start, and we can make of it what we want, write what we want on that blank canvas. Keeping that enthusiasm going can be tough—a bit like trying to take up exercise. The first few times are impossibly hard, but if you persevere, then one day you find you're jogging, walking, swimming without conscious effort. But getting going is really tough and requires immense powers of concentration, enthusiasm, dedication, and perseverance to keep at it.

Try to see the past as a room separate from the one you live in now. You can go in there, but you don't live there anymore. You can go visit, but it isn't home any more. Home is here now. Each second of this present is precious. Don't waste any drops of precious time by spending too much time in that old room. Don't miss what is happening now because you were too busy looking back, or later you'll be busy looking back at this time and wondering why you wasted it. Live here, live now, live in this moment.

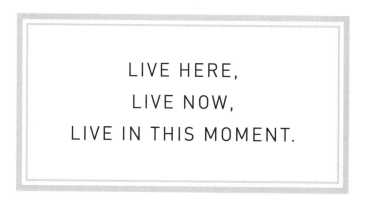

LIVE HERE,
LIVE NOW,
LIVE IN THIS MOMENT.

# RULE 23

# Don't Live in the Future

Heck, if you thought the previous Rule was tough, try this one ... But the future is where it's all going to happen, I hear you cry. The future is where I'm going to be successful, happy, rich, beautiful, famous, in love, in work, out of this crap relationship, out on the town, surrounded by friends, surrounded by the finest wines money can buy. Yep, those might be plans or dreams or whatever. But again, this here and now is where it is actually at. This is the moment you've been waiting for all your life. This is the moment you must appreciate without all those other things you long for. Look, longing really is the sweetest thing. Having those dreams is brilliant. Don't let anyone ever tell you dreaming is a bad thing. But appreciate that it is the you right now that is doing the dreaming. Enjoy the wishing and the longing. Enjoy being alive and having the strength and vitality to do all that dreaming.

Living in the moment doesn't mean throwing away all your responsibilities and cares; it doesn't mean taking off and being a total pleasure seeker; it doesn't mean sitting cross-legged and breathing deeply—although all and any of these things is fine if you want. It just means taking a moment or two every now and then to appreciate being alive and to aim to act like today matters and live life to the full, right here, right now.

We can't project all our future happiness into the future—"Oh if only I were richer/younger/healthier/happier/more in love/less in this relationship/had a better job/had nicer children/had a better car/were slimmer/taller/fitter/had more hair/better teeth/more clothes"—the list is endless. If only this or that was changed everything would be perfect, wouldn't it? Unfortunately not—it just doesn't work like that. When this and that gets changed, there will always be something else, waiting its turn and putting off that happiness until some later date. If you were to suddenly find that you were slimmer/fitter or whatever, then you'd probably find yourself wanting to be richer or that your partner was more loving. You'd find other things to wish for to make you happy.

Forget bigger and better and richer and thinner. The key is to appreciate what we've got right now and yet still dream and plan. That way we'll be a little happier now than if we're constantly looking to the future, where happiness apparently lies.

And don't go thinking it's all right for me; it's not. I too, need to lose a few pounds, certainly get fitter, get more stuff (and how we all love stuff). But I also value the way I am and appreciate what I've got right now because—and this is the secret—it is real. The me that is now is the real me; the future one isn't yet born and may not happen. (You mean I might not lose that extra weight or get fitter? Yep, right.) And the stuff I have now is at least real, tangible, solid. Dreams are great, but reality is fine, too.

DREAMS ARE GREAT, BUT
REALITY IS FINE, TOO.

# RULE 24

# Get On with Life—
# It's Whooshing Past

Every day, every second, life is whooshing past at an alarming rate. And it goes on getting faster and faster. I once asked an 84-year-old man if life slowed down as you got older. His reply was unprintable, but he explained to me in no uncertain terms that no, it didn't. It carried on getting faster. I sometimes wonder if we aren't picking up speed for take-off, if you know what I mean—a sort of trial run before we leave. But the Rule, if you want your life to be successful, happy, fulfilled, meaningful, jam-packed with adventure and reward, is to simply get on with it. And I'm sure you do, or you wouldn't be reading this.

So, how do we get on with it? Well, the easiest way is the same way we would get on with anything else we knew we had to do. We start with setting a target (a goal, an objective), make a plan, formulate a set of actions to take us toward the target, and then, well, get on with it.

Imagine you were a project manager for a big company that wanted you to organize, say, an exhibition. You would begin with clarifying what you wanted from the exhibition, what it was supposed to achieve (for example, to sell 100 items or to give away free gifts or to drum up 20 new customers). This gives you something to aim for. Then you would formulate your plan—booking the stand, arranging the staff, getting stuff printed, etc. With the plan in place, you would work out what you needed and then get on with it.

Life isn't so different. It's a project—albeit on a vast scale and much more important than an exhibition stand.

# RULE 24

I'm sure you get the idea. You have to get on with life, but it is so easy to wallow if you don't have a goal (or goals) and a plan. It's very easy for the days to blur into each other if you've no idea where you are going or what you want to achieve.

None of this, by the way, need take away any spontaneity from life if that's what you're thinking. I don't regard life like a work project, honestly. I do see it as a challenging, rewarding, exciting, rich and diverse, unexpected, and rather fantastic experience. But you have to give it a bit of thought if you want to get the best out of it. Without that thought, the days will blur. Without that thought, it's easy to find yourself adrift—floating downstream.

I used to think that whatever turned up would be fine. I was a sort of adventurous fatalist—I would be ready for whatever challenge was thrown my way. But, increasingly, I see the huge advantage of having a goal and working toward that rather than drifting aimlessly. It makes it so much easier for good things to happen.

YOU HAVE TO GIVE IT
A BIT OF THOUGHT IF YOU
WANT TO GET THE BEST
OUT OF IT.

# Be Consistent

I had an email from a reader of the first edition of this book, who pointed out that an example I gave in one of the Rules in this book was in breach of another Rule. Nope, I'm not going to tell you which one. You'll have to work it out for yourself like he did.

In my defense, I'd like to point out that this means I was following the Rule about not being perfect. However, there's no denying that the reader in question had me figured out and, as he observed (very politely I must say), it's important to be consistent.

Well, I've never been arrogant (or stupid) enough to claim that I never break any of the Rules. After all, they're Rules that I know work from observing other people, not a list of personal preferences. So I try to follow them as closely as I can, and the older I get the more often I get, it right. But that's not the same as always.

However, we certainly should aim to be consistent about following whatever Rules we decide to live by (the ones in this book and/or any others). There's no point in choosing a path if you're just going to wander off it at whim.

I find that my children are a big help here*. (If you don't have kids, you'll have to work that bit harder to identify your own inconsistencies.) If you're debating a point of disagreement with the children (yes, that is indeed a euphemism), you can rely on them to draw your attention to any inconsistencies in your line of argument, or indeed any inconsistencies between what you're telling them now and what you did yourself

* See! I always knew they'd come in handy for something.

yesterday. It's a fine line between inconsistency and hypocrisy, and the more clear we are about what we believe and why, the easier it is to be consistent in what we think, say, and do.

For example, suppose your son points out that you criticize him if he complains about classmates behind their backs, but you were moaning about a colleague on the phone to your mom last night. You may need to think about the difference between complaining and having a much-needed moan, and then make sure you're consistent—with yourself as well as your child—about what you allow.

And here's another thing. It makes life easier for everybody else if you are consistent. Erratic people are difficult to live with and be around. So are moody people. If your friends and family don't know how you'll react to the same event or suggestion from one day to the next, you make them live their lives on edge. Unless you are a hermit. I'm not talking about being predictable and boring. Your ideas and activities and enthusiasms can be wonderfully unpredictable and fascinating. It's just your behavior toward other people that needs to be reliable and consistent. You have the potential to make people's lives richer and easier and better—or darker and trickier and more exhausting. Which do you choose?

> THERE'S NO POINT IN
> CHOOSING A PATH IF
> YOU'RE JUST GOING TO
> WANDER OFF IT AT WHIM.

# RULE 26

# Dress Like Today Is Important

Today is important. It is the only day you've got that has some reality to it. Why shouldn't you treat it as important? It is. So dress like it matters. And no, I don't mean in the way my mother always used to tell me, "Make sure you've got clean underwear on; you never know when you'll get run over by a bus." I loved this as a kid. I couldn't see how important clean underwear would really be if I were lying there in the road. And I used to imagine how, if my parents got me to the hospital in time and the doctor stripped away my torn and blood-soaked trousers, he'd look down and gasp in horror, "Don't look! This kid has got yesterday's pants on—get him out of here!"

Look, a lot of these Rules are about conscious choice, conscious decisions, conscious awareness. Those I have observed who seem to have a handle on this thing called life are conscious people. They are awake and aware. They know what they are doing and where they are going. If you, too, want your life to be more than a set of random events that happen to you and instead make it a series of stimulating challenges and rewarding and enriching experiences, then you, too, have to be conscious.

And you do this by greeting each day as if it is important. You get up and shower/wash/shave/put on make-up/comb hair/brush teeth, etc. to make you look good, feel good, smell good. And then you dress smartly, cleanly, snappily, stylishly, as if you were going to a job interview or a birthday party or an outing. If you dress for each day expectantly, importantly, smartly, then each day will become that.

People will react differently to you if you dress as if it matters—and you'll react differently to that different reaction. It's an upward spiral. I have to stress we're not talking formal here; you don't have to be buttoned up and uncomfortable. Just dress as if it matters.

But what about weekends, I hear you ask, surely we can relax then? Of course, but it doesn't mean you should let yourself go. On weekends you're going to see friends and/or family (unless you spend every weekend totally alone), and they, too, deserve to see you looking good, and as if they matter. Hey, not even your friends want to see you slovenly, dishevelled, untidy, uncared for. But this bit is really about you. If you greet each day as if it is important, then it will do wonders to your self-esteem, your self-respect, your self-confidence.

But, hey, I don't want you taking anything on trust. Try dressing like today matters and see what happens. If you don't perk up and feel completely different within a fortnight, then go back to your old ways and to hell with this Rule. But I can guarantee you'll feel great and face each day livelier and more energetic and happier.

If you adopt the conscious approach to living, you'll find it quite hard to consciously dress down.

PEOPLE WILL REACT
DIFFERENTLY TO YOU
IF YOU DRESS AS IF
IT MATTERS.

# Have a Belief System

No, no, no, this isn't where I begin a religious rant or a New Age indoctrination process to welcome you into a strange cult. This is where I simply say that those who have a belief system to sustain them through times of crisis and trouble do better than those who don't. It's that simple.

Now what do we mean by a belief system? Ah, that's harder to put into words. I guess a belief system is what you think the world is all about—the universe and everything. It's what you believe will happen to you after you die. It's what or who you pray to when the night is dark and you are in trouble. Those who have a handle on this curious thing called life seem to be the ones who have worked out, satisfactorily for themselves at least, what they think it's all about. And it doesn't seem to matter what it is they think that is. You could believe in God or many gods, or you could believe in something or someone else—maybe that we're all the product of some weird alien experiment, or you might be a fervent flat earther—it doesn't matter. Well, I guess it will to you, but as long as you have a belief system, you will do better than those who don't. Being a seeker is not conducive to having a happy life.

I know you're going to say, "But what if I haven't been able to find an answer and don't have a belief system? What am I supposed to do then?" Why, carry on looking, I guess, but do try to wrap this one up pretty quick, as it's an important Rule. Put aside some time to think about it, and make sure you put it high on your list of priorities.

I hope you notice I'm not giving you any advice here as to what sort of belief system to have. Any one will do as long as it supports you in times of trouble, answers your questions about your life and what you mean to the universe, and gives you comfort.

You have to be comfortable with your belief system; it's no good having one in which a vengeful and violent deity watches your every move and terrifies you into submission. (Sorry, if you've already got one like that, you might need to rethink it.)

You might want to think about whether your belief system makes you feel guilt-ridden or unhappy, asks you to cut bits off your body or in any way mutilate or change your appearance, excludes anyone else on the basis of their race or sex, or needs any formal ritual to bring you the comfort it promises. For some, the ideal belief system won't have any sort of figurehead who needs worshipping, obeying, or submitting to in any way, shape, or form. This is personal, but it's worth thinking about what you are OK with.

A belief system has to be that—a belief. You don't have to prove it to anyone else, justify it, [or] show it (see Rule 1), convert anyone else to it, or preach to the world in general. You may feel free to take bits from all other belief systems to build your own. But if you can, have something.

YOU DON'T HAVE TO PROVE
IT TO ANYONE ELSE,
JUSTIFY IT,
[OR] SHOW IT.

# Leave a Little Space for Yourself Each Day

Most people think they get this, but most people might be wrong. You may think you have a little quality time each day for yourself, but I bet you don't. You see, even in our time alone, we spend so much of it worrying about others, caring for our family, friends, and loved ones, that there is very little left over entirely for ourselves. What I am proposing isn't revolutionary or difficult or extreme. In fact, it's pretty easy. Just leave a little space for yourself each day. Perhaps only ten minutes (ideally half an hour) put aside and devoted entirely to yourself. Selfish? You bet. Of course it is and justifiably so— you are the captain, the engine, the driving force, the motivator, the rock. You need that time to regenerate, renew, invigorate yourself. You need that downtime to recharge and repair. If you don't, you aren't taking on fresh fuel. Your engine will run down, and so will you.

So what are you going to do with that time? Answer: absolutely nothing. And I do mean nothing. This isn't time for lying in the bath, sitting on the toilet, meditating, reading the newspapers, or sleeping. This is a little space for you, a breather, a time to sit still and do absolutely nothing. Just breathe. I find that ten minutes sitting in the garden just breathing is a fantastic boost a couple of times a day. I sit there, not thinking, not doing, not worrying, just being, while I appreciate the pleasure of being alive.

I discovered this Rule when I was a teenager. I found it invaluable as a way of purging myself of angst and worries. My mother used to call out to me, "What are you doing?" To which the reply was inevitably, "Nothing." And she would always reply, "Well come in here, and I'll find you something to do." She also used to say, "You'll never amount to anything by having your head stuck in a book." And the one I loved the most: "No one needs to think as much as you do." How do you answer that?

I find time spent doing nothing really important, and as soon as I complicate it, it loses something. If I add a cup of coffee to my solitude, then it's a coffee break and not a space just for me. If I listen to music, then it's a music break. If I have a companion with me and I chat, then it's a social occasion. If I read the papers then I have moved away entirely from the concept of a little space for me. Keep it simple. Keep it bare. Keep it pure.

> IT IS THE LITTLE SPACE
> JUST FOR YOURSELF
> WHILE YOU DO
> ABSOLUTELY NOTHING.

# RULE 29

## Have a Plan

You've got to have a plan. A plan is a map, a guide, a target, a focus, a route, a signpost, a direction, a path, a strategy. It says that you are going to go somewhere, do something, be somewhere by a certain time. It gives your life structure and shape, gravitas, and power. If you allow life to turn up any old thing, you'll be floating downstream as quick as you like. OK, so not all plans work out, and not all maps lead to the treasure. But at least you're in with a better chance if you have a map and a shovel than if you just dig at random—or, like most people, don't dig at all.

A plan indicates you've thought about your life and aren't just waiting for something to turn up. Or, again like most people, you're not even thinking about it but going through life perpetually surprised by what happens. Work out what it is you want to do, plan it, work out the steps to take to achieve your goal, and get on with it. If you don't plan your plan, it will remain a dream.

So what happens if you don't have a plan? Well, you reinforce, to yourself, your sense of being "not in control." Once you have a plan, everything else falls into place. Once you have a plan, the logical steps to achieve that plan also become available, accessible.

A plan isn't a dream—it's something you intend to do rather than something you want to do. And having a plan means you've thought through how you're going to do it.

Of course, just because you have a plan doesn't mean that you have to stick to it, or follow it to the letter come hell or high water. The plan is always up for review, for improvement, for changing as and when you need to. The plan shouldn't be rigid. Circumstances change, you change, your plan changes. The details of the plan don't matter. Having one does.

Having a plan gives you a fall-back position. When life gets hectic—and boy does it do that sometimes—it is easy to forget what we are here for. Having a plan means that when the dust settles, you can remember, "Now what was I doing? Oh yes, I remember. My plan was to...." And off you go again, back on course.

IF YOU DON'T PLAN
YOUR PLAN, IT WILL
REMAIN A DREAM.

# RULE 30

## Have a Sense of Humor

How important this is. As we struggle through this life—and it can be a struggle—we need to keep a sense of proportion about it. What we do and what we take seriously can often be so far removed from what it is actually all about that it is laughable. We get bogged down in trivia, lost in irrelevant detail to such an extent that our life can whizz past and we don't even notice. By letting go of things that really aren't important, we can put ourselves back on the right track. And the best way to do that is through humor—laughing at ourselves, laughing at our situation, but never laughing at others—they're just as lost as we are and don't need to be laughed at.

We get bogged down in things like worrying what the neighbors will think, concerns over stuff we don't have, or things we haven't done: "Oh no, I haven't washed the car for two weeks, and it's filthy. Next door did theirs yesterday, so it looks like we are really slovenly." If we ever think we're getting like that, then we do need to have a laugh about it. Life is for living, enjoying the sunshine, big things—not getting in a terrible state because you dropped some eggs on the supermarket floor.

Laughing at yourself and situations you find yourself in has a double positive effect. First, it diffuses tension and helps regain a sense of proportion. Second, it has real physical as well as mental benefits. Laughter causes the release of endorphins, which make you feel better as well as give you a better perspective on life.

# RULE 30

This isn't about telling jokes all the time or cracking witty puns. It's more being able to see something funny in whatever life throws at us along the way—and there is always some humor in everything. I once came round after being unconscious from a serious car crash. I was in a cubicle in a hospital and in great pain. As I regained consciousness, I let out a couple of choice words to describe my condition and, as I did so, the nurse arrived and opened the curtains only for me to find a nun sat outside.* I was mortified and immediately apologized. She looked at me most gravely, winked, and quietly said, "It's OK. I've said worse myself."

If you observe any aspect of human behavior, you can see the ridiculousness in all of it. Learn to find the funny side of everything. It's the best technique for instant stress relief and dissolves anxiety and doubt. Try it.

> SEE SOMETHING FUNNY IN WHATEVER LIFE THROWS AT [YOU] ALONG THE WAY.

* Nothing to do with me! She was quietly waiting for another nun who was being checked out for a splinter in her finger, I later discovered.

# RULE 31

## Choose How You Make Your Bed

Every action you take, every decision you make, everything you do causes an immediate effect on those around you—and on you. And this is the important bit. There is such a thing as instant karma. It is your bed, and you are going to have to lie in it. Your actions will dictate whether in general your life is going to run happily or badly, smoothly or as if the wheels have fallen off. If you are selfish and manipulative, it will rebound on you. If you are generally loving and thoughtful, you will get your just rewards—and not in heaven (or the next life or whatever you believe) but right here, right now.

Trust me. Whatever you do and how you do it will come back to you in spades. This isn't a threat, merely an observation. Those who do good, get good. Those who do bad, get bad.

I know we can all point to people who seem to have it made and are still pretty vile. But they don't sleep at night. They have no one to really love them. Inside they are sad and lonely and frightened. Those who go around sharing a bit of love and kindness get rewarded with the same coming back.

It's a bit like the old adage that "You are what you eat." You are what you do. Look at the faces of those who spread joy, and you will see laughter lines and smiles. Look at those who like to bully, get their own way, and are arrogant or demanding or vicious, and you will see etched lines of misery and fear and frowns where there ought to be lightness. These lines won't ever be taken away by face creams or suntans or plastic surgery. They are what they do, and you can see it in their eyes—and the state of their bed, of course.

So be careful how you make your bed. What goes around comes around. There is instant karma. What you sow you reap. Better to stand up and be counted right from the start. Do the right thing every time. You know what it is. Then when you get in the bed you've made, not only will you be able to sleep at night, but you'll sleep the sleep of the just.

DO THE RIGHT THING
EVERY TIME.
YOU KNOW WHAT IT IS.

# Life Can Be a Bit Like Advertising

Someone once said that half of the money he spent on advertising was wasted, but he didn't know which half.* His point was, of course, that if you can't tell which half, then you have to keep on doing the whole lot, fully aware that not all of it will produce rewards. Life is a bit like that. Sometimes it seems so unfair. You put in loads of effort and get nothing back. You're polite to people and everyone seems rude back. You work up a sweat and others cruise it. Well, you have to keep on doing the 100 percent because you don't know which bits will pay off. I know it isn't fair, but then life isn't. Your efforts will be rewarded eventually, but you'll probably never know which efforts are being rewarded—or for what—and which aren't.

We tend to think we are being lucky sometimes when actually we are just being rewarded for some bit of effort long ago that we have forgotten about. We have to keep going. You can't give up on the grounds that you've had a setback or two, because you don't know which setbacks are the ones that count and which ones aren't. I suppose it's like the number of frogs you have to get acquainted with before you find your prince (or princess). Or the pile of oysters you'd have to open to find a pearl.

But whatever you do, don't lose heart because things don't seem to be panning out. Only by keeping up the effort will rewards come in eventually—and you'll never know from which bits come the best reward.

*Lord Leverhulme, I believe.

Most well-balanced and happy people will also tell you that sometimes you have to work at something without looking for a payoff—apart from the immediate payoff that we are being kept busy and thus can't get into trouble. Always looking for success, rewards, a payoff can be detrimental to our well-being when things don't pan out. Sometimes it's OK to do things just for the sheer enjoyment of doing them. I love painting miniature watercolors—tiny, tiny landscapes. Once in a while someone will come along and suggest I put them into an exhibition or sell them commercially. And every time I do it fails miserably, and I give up for a while. Once the dust has settled, I always go back to them. I have learned it is a personal thing, and no longer will I try to sell them or show them. They are a not-for-profit part of my life and immensely rewarding. No, you can't see one.

YOU'LL NEVER KNOW
FROM WHICH BITS OF
EFFORT COME THE
BEST REWARD.

# Get Used to Stepping Outside Your Comfort Zone

Be prepared to be a little bit brave every day. Why? Because if you don't you'll grow stagnant and moldy or curl up and wither. We all have a comfort zone where we feel safe and warm and dry. But every now and then we need to step outside and be challenged, be frightened, be stimulated. It's this way that we stay young and feel good about ourselves.

If we grow too attached to our comfort zone, chances are it will start to shrink, or something will come along and dismantle it. Fate, or whatever it is that runs things, doesn't like us to get too complacent, and every now and then it gives us a great big cosmic kick up the backside to wake us up. If we have practiced stretching the boundaries of our woolly cocoon occasionally, that kick won't have too much impact—we're ready for it—it's much easier to cope.

But it's more than that. Expanding your comfort zone makes you feel good about yourself. It gives you extra confidence. And the best bit is that you can do it oh so gently. You don't have to go hang gliding or fire walking or have sex with a stranger just to test your comfort zone. It might be as simple as volunteering for something that you've never done before and that you feel slightly nervous about. It could be taking up a new sport or hobby. Maybe it will involve joining something. It could be doing something alone that you've only ever done in company before or speaking up for yourself when you would usually keep quiet.

We impose a lot of restrictions on ourselves that limit us, hold us back. We think we couldn't do that, wouldn't feel happy with that. Taking the challenge of expanding our comfort zone brings us out of ourselves and keeps us learning and growing. You can't grow mold if you're growing experience.

EXPANDING YOUR
COMFORT ZONE MAKES
YOU FEEL GOOD ABOUT
YOURSELF.

# RULE 34

# Learn to Ask Questions

Look, you may not like the answers, but at least you'll know. Most of the world's problems can be laid firmly at the feet of assumptions. If we assume (no, I'm not going to do that dreadful "it makes an ass out of u and me" stuff*) then, in effect, we think we know but we don't. We assume that our bit of faulty information is a fact, and things go on getting worse. We assume that other people like our plan but they don't, and it all goes pear-shaped. Better to ask questions right from the start and know what's what.

Questions help clarify the situation. Questions put people on the spot, which means they have to think—and thinking is always a good thing for everybody about everything. Questions help people clarify their thoughts. Questions demand answers, and answers require the situation to be thought through, to its logical conclusion.

As someone very wise and very dear to me once said, "The better you understand the beliefs, actions, desires, and wants of others, the more likely you are to make the right response, alter your own thinking where necessary, and generally be successful."

Asking questions gives you time to think, buys you breathing space. Rather than flying off the handle because you think you know the situation, it's better to ask a few questions and find out the truth. You'll be better equipped to respond logically, calmly, and correctly.

*I know I did but that was a joke.

You can always tell the real Rules Players; they're the ones asking questions while others are reacting, panicking, misinterpreting, assuming, losing control, and generally behaving badly.

Ask questions of yourself constantly. Ask why you think you're right—or wrong. Ask yourself why you are doing certain things, want other things, follow a particular course of action. Question yourself firmly and rigorously, because maybe there isn't anyone else doing it. And you need it. We all do. It keeps us from assuming we know what's best for ourselves.

And, of course, there is a time to stop asking questions—of others and of ourselves. You have to know when to back off. All this takes a long time to learn, and we all make mistakes as we go. Any questions?

QUESTIONS HELP PEOPLE
CLARIFY THEIR THOUGHTS.

# Have Dignity

I've spent years watching successful people, and I don't just mean successful as in having lots of money or a big-shot career. In fact, one of the most successful people I ever met lived incredibly frugally, simply, and reclusively and yet had cracked success in a really big way—happiness, peace, contentment. This was a person you couldn't have wiped the inner smile off even if you had tried.

Almost all successful people have a sense of their own dignity. Now what do I mean by this? Well, they are all pretty solid in themselves; they have worked out who they are and what they are about. They don't need to show off or brag about what they have or who they are. They don't need to draw attention to themselves because they aren't particularly interested in what we think—they are too busy getting on with things in their own lives. They maintain decorum (lovely old-fashioned word) not because they are frightened of making a fool of themselves or falling flat on their face but because they simply can't be bothered with attention-seeking stuff.

It is important—if you want to be a successful Rules Player— to show poise and gravitas, be a bit separate from the herd, have good manners, be polite and considerate, and be someone others might like to look up to. You don't have to be all aloof and stand-offish, serious and grown-up. You can still have fun—just don't go making an idiot of yourself. You can still let your hair down—just don't let go of control completely. You can still relax—just don't fall off the edge.

# RULE 35

Dignity is about showing self-respect and having quiet self-esteem. It's amazing how others will respect you and hold you in greater esteem when you start the ball rolling.

DIGNITY IS ABOUT
SHOWING SELF-RESPECT
AND HAVING QUIET
SELF-ESTEEM.

# RULE 36

## It's OK to Feel Big Emotions

If we're busily maintaining dignity and being peaceful, it's tempting to think that we're detached, and there's no place for big feelings. Well, the good news is, it doesn't work like that. It is OK to feel emotions. It is OK to feel angry when someone really upsets you. It is OK to feel huge sadness and grief when you lose a loved one. It is OK to feel tremendous joy. It is OK to be scared, anxious, relieved, excited, apprehensive, and all the others.

We are human beings, and we have emotions. This is all quite natural. It is quite natural to feel big things deeply, and it's OK to let it all show. We don't have to be ashamed of our feelings. It is OK to cry. Sitting on our feelings isn't a good idea. They just get squashed that way. It's far better to let them out, deal with them, and then get on with things.

If we go through trauma, upsetting experiences, and difficult times, it certainly doesn't help to be thinking all the time that we have to keep a lid on it or people will think us weak or out of control. I know this might look as if it contradicts keeping our dignity, but feeling emotion is not undignified unless we express it inappropriately or at the wrong time.

Sometimes even getting angry is totally appropriate—as long as we remain in control and don't do anything we might regret later. Getting angry reminds people that we aren't a pushover and that they have hurt/offended/threatened us deeply and seriously and that their actions have caused us great pain. Of course, we shouldn't get angry over silly things—instead, we should choose to show anger only when it is needed, and needed seriously. Likewise, it's not good to get angry and take it out on innocent people—if you can't express the anger appropriately, then you need to find a way of letting it out that isn't going to hurt anybody else. But let it out you must. Bottled anger eats away at you.

It's not just anger that shouldn't be permanently restrained. Neither should fear or anxiety or great joy or any of the other emotions. Just because we are feeling big emotions doesn't mean we are out of control. We can be quite emotional and still be in charge of what we are expressing. You wouldn't be human if you didn't feel stuff—and feel it big time. Emotions are natural, and you shouldn't make an attempt to stifle them. Of course, you can make sure emotion is let out at an appropriate time and place, but that is within your control. But then again if you do respond badly, you can always feel guilty about it afterward—and that's OK, too.

> SITTING ON OUR FEELINGS
> ISN'T A GOOD IDEA.
> THEY JUST GET SQUASHED
> THAT WAY.

# RULE 37

## Keep the Faith

Keeping the faith is about sticking to your promises, going down into darkness rose-crowned, proud, and unreluctant, knowing you've done the right thing and stuck by your friends in times of trouble. These are perhaps old-fashioned values— honor, loyalty, trust, pride, support, fidelity, reliability, dependability, strength, seeing things through, constancy—but no less worth having for all that. We live in a throw-away society, and keeping your word, being there when you said you would, being dependable and reliable, makes you stand out as a person of some value, some worth. This is a good thing.

We fight shy of being "good" these days in case people mistake us for "goody-goodies." But that's another thing entirely. Keeping the faith is something you do. Being a goody-goody is when you try to convert others. Having your own values and keeping them to yourself (sticking to Rule 1) is fine. Trying to make everyone else do the same as you is a bad thing. That makes you a goody-goody.

No, it doesn't apply to me because I'm only giving out information, not trying to convert you. It is entirely up to you whether you pick up this information and run with it. But I can guarantee you I shall keep the faith, and the information I give you today will be the same information I would give you in 20 years' time. Old-fashioned values never go out of style (perhaps they've always been out), and I shan't let you down.

KEEPING THE FAITH IS
SOMETHING YOU DO.
BEING A GOODY-GOODY IS
WHEN YOU TRY TO
CONVERT OTHERS.

# You'll Never Understand Everything

Look, we are tiny complex humans in a huge complex world (and even bigger universe). It's all so unimaginably, fantastically strange that, believe me, we'll never be able to understand everything. And that applies at all levels and in all areas of life. Once you grasp this rule, you'll sleep easier at night.

There are likely to be a few things going on around you right now, as there always will be, that will remain just slightly outside of your comprehension. People will behave oddly and you won't understand why. Things will go unexpectedly wrong— or right—and it won't make sense. Spend all your time desperately trying to work it all out and you'll drive yourself crazy. Much better to just accept that there is always stuff that we won't understand and let it go at that. How simple that is.

It's the same principle for the big stuff—why things happen to us, why we are here, where we go afterward, that sort of thing. Some of it we'll never know, some of it we can try and work out, but I have a sneaking feeling it won't turn out to be anything like we think.

It's as if our lives are an enormous jigsaw and all we get access to is the bottom-left bit. And from that we make these huge assumptions: "Oh, it's a ...." But when the veil gets taken away, we see that the jigsaw is massive and that the one tiny bit we were scrutinizing was actually something else, and there we are looking at an entirely different picture than the one we'd imagined.

We are now collecting information faster than any human, or any computer, can process it. We can't understand it all. We can't even begin to understand a tiny fraction of it. Same with our lives. Stuff is going on around us at such a rate we'll never get to the bottom of it. Because as fast as we try, the picture changes, new information comes in, and our understanding alters.

Be curious, ask questions, wonder to yourself, talk to other people if you like—but know that this won't always give you a clear and concrete answer. People don't always make sense. Life doesn't always make sense. Let it go, and discover the peace of mind that comes with knowing that you'll never understand everything. Sometimes it just is.

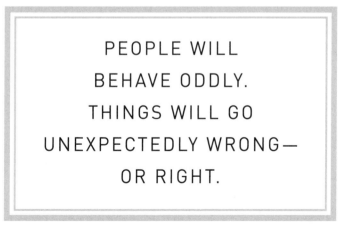

PEOPLE WILL
BEHAVE ODDLY.
THINGS WILL GO
UNEXPECTEDLY WRONG—
OR RIGHT.

# Know Where True Happiness
# Comes From

No, I'm not about to reveal the secret people have sought since the beginning of time—where true happiness comes from. But I do know where it isn't to be found. And I do have an inkling where it might be. Let's take a scenario. You go out to buy a new car/house/suit/computer/whatever turns you on. You have the money (no, I have no idea where you get it from; this is just an example) and you buy whatever it is, and it makes you feel incredible/happy/excited/fantastic. Now imagine whoever it was who built/made/created whatever it is you bought. When that person made it, where did he fit that feeling in? I think you might have brought that feeling with you.

Now imagine you fall in love. It is incredible. You feel fantastic, happy, excited. You go to meet your new love, and when you see him, that feeling spills out in all directions. You feel amazing because you are with him and he is generating that feeling. Right? Wrong. Again, you brought it all with you. You may look to him to trigger it, but even if he went to the other end of the planet, you'll still have that feeling.

You get fired. Ghastly. You are given your papers. You walk away devastated. You feel like nothing. Now where in that documentation is that feeling you now have? Nowhere, that's right. Again, you brought it all with you. We all go to work every day with the potential to have that "I've just been fired" feeling. We all meet new people with the "I've fallen head over heels in love" feeling.

But no amount of falling in love, buying new stuff, or getting sacked is going to keep that feeling going for longer than it takes us to get over it. People get addicted to buying new stuff or falling in love or whatever because they just love that feeling without realizing that they already have it. They have to keep having their "fix" because they think it's the only way to get that feeling going. The secret is knowing how to trigger it without anyone else or anything else being involved. No, I don't know. You have to find that one for yourself. Clue: It's the one place you'd never think of looking—yep, right inside you.

I THINK YOU MIGHT HAVE
BROUGHT THAT FEELING
WITH YOU.

# Life Is a Pizza

I love my kids. I love reading to them, playing with them, watching them grow up, listening to them talk, teaching them to ride bikes, taking them to the beach, and generally hanging out with them.

Mind you, I hate picking up after them, listening to them squabble, and being spoken to in that dismissive way that only teenagers can really do justice to. But I can't seem to have the good bits without the picking up, the squabbles, and the sharp end of a teenager's tongue from time to time. I wouldn't be without them, though (most days).

I love pizza, too. I love crispy pizzas, and I like the soft squishy ones. Any pizza really. I love peperoni and mozzarella and tomatoes and juicy chunks of ham and piquant capers and crispy onions. Mind you, I hate olives, and they sometimes appear on pizzas without being ordered. Disgraceful. And those dried up tomatoes you sometimes get. The ones that are all chewy. Ugh! I always pick those off and throw them away.

When my kids were little, they'd refuse to eat a pizza that had something they didn't like on it. They'd burst into tears and sob, "I hate mushrooms!" or "I can't stand cooked tomatoes!" They had to learn that, if they couldn't work round the mushrooms or cooked tomatoes, they couldn't have pizza at all.

You know what I'm going to say. Yes, life is a pizza, with everything on it. If you want the good bits, you have to deal with the bad bits. If you love everything about your job apart from one person you don't like dealing with, recognize that the job comes as a package and you buy into it or quit the job. If you love your partner but hate the way she sulks after an arguement, accept her as she is and recognize that the sulking is the bit that reminds you how wonderful everything else is. If your neighbor is friendly and keeps an eye on your property when you're out and signs for your deliveries and babysits the kids, you just have to live with the fact that she talks too much; and stop moaning about it. And when you stop moaning, you'll probably find you mind it much less.

I know parents who move their child from school to school until they find one that's perfect in every way. They never do find that, of course, but eventually they have to stop because the child has grown up. I'm not saying you should never move your child (if you have the option), but stop looking for perfection because you won't find it. Life isn't perfect.

The best things in life come with chewy, dried tomatoes and olives. There's no point moaning. Just pick them off, or swallow them down as fast as you can, and then sink your teeth into what's left and relish every bite.

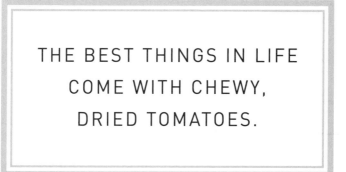

THE BEST THINGS IN LIFE
COME WITH CHEWY,
DRIED TOMATOES.

# RULE 41

## Know When to Let Go—
## When to Walk Away

Sometimes you have to just walk away. We all hate to fail, hate to give up, hate to give in. We love the challenge of life and want to keep on until whatever we are trying to "win" has been overcome, vanquished, beaten, won. But sometimes it just ain't going to happen, and we need to learn to recognize those moments, learn how to philosophically shrug and walk away with our pride intact and our dignity high.

Sometimes you really want to do something, but it is unrealistic. Instead of knocking yourself out, cultivate the art of knowing when to walk away, and you'll find it a lot less stressful.

If a relationship is coming to its end, instead of playing out long and complicated—and potentially hurtful—end games, learn the art of walking away. If it's dead, leave it. This isn't a Rule that should be in the relationship section—it's here because it is for *you*, to protect you, to nurture you. This is nothing to do with "them" but all to do with you. If it's dead, don't go digging it up every five minutes to check if there's a pulse. It's dead; walk away.

You may want to get even. Don't get mad; walk away. This is much better than getting even because it shows you have risen above whatever it is that is driving you crazy. And there can be no better way of getting even than to ignore something so completely it can be left behind.

Letting go and walking away means you are exercising control and good decision-making powers—you are making your choice rather than letting the situation control you.

I don't want to be rude, but your problems—hey, my problems, too—won't even warrant a footnote in the history of the universe. Walk away now and look back after ten years. I bet you'll be hard pressed to even remember what it was all about. No, this isn't a "time is the best healer" crusade, but putting space and time between you and your troubles does give you a wider view, a better perspective. And the way to do that is to walk away, put that space there. Time will put itself there, in time.

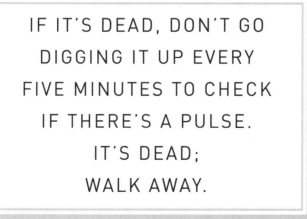

IF IT'S DEAD, DON'T GO
DIGGING IT UP EVERY
FIVE MINUTES TO CHECK
IF THERE'S A PULSE.
IT'S DEAD;
WALK AWAY.

# RULE 42

## Retaliation Leads to Escalation

Now, I'll be honest here. Among my friends, I'm not actually known for my tolerance or my ability to let things lie. Frankly, if someone puts me down or winds me up, my first instinct is to respond in kind. When I was (much) younger, this led to the occasional fist fight. Even when I learned to stop picking fights—or letting other people pick them with me—I still couldn't resist a smartass retort or a petty act of vengeance.

Well, it's hard. If your neighbor cuts down a tree that's technically yours, you feel aggrieved and want to cut down one of his trees that overhangs your fence—even if you didn't particularly like the original tree. Or perhaps a colleague at work takes credit for an idea that you came up with. How tempting to get her back by forgetting to mention until the last minute that the deadline on her current project is being brought forward, or drawing attention to the fact that last month's catastrophic exhibition was her idea.

However, think about it. (After many years even I learned to think this one through, so I'm sure you can.) Anyone who is prepared to cut down your tree or steal your idea isn't about to take your little act of revenge lying down. Nope. This person is going to bulldoze your garage next, or try to get you fired. Then what'll you do? Blow up his car? Hire an employment lawyer? Are you sure this isn't getting out of hand?

Actually, this is one lesson I learned from my kids.\* The thing about siblings is that they're so upfront with their squabbles that you can watch the whole thing spiral out of control much faster than in grown-up versions. We so-called adults plot and

\*And I've been trying to teach it back to them ever since.

scheme and plan our Machiavellian strategies over days or even months.

Brothers and sisters can go from a minor disagreement to all-out war within minutes.

Look, retaliation can only lead to one thing—an escalation of hostilities. That's the story of wars the world over and throughout history. And we're no different in our dealings with neighbors, colleagues, and all those other people we get thrown together with whether we like them or not.

So how do we call an end to this madness? The cycle is only broken when one of those involved is mature enough to see that someone has got to bite her tongue, or hold back, to stop it in its tracks. Someone has to be grown-up enough to turn the other cheek, assume the moral high ground, take it like a man**, call a halt, and just let the whole thing drop. Yes, even when you have got a really cutting retort, or cunning masterstroke up your sleeve. It really is sometimes better to do nothing, say nothing. Come on, if I can do it, anyone can.

> ANYONE WHO IS PREPARED
> TO CUT DOWN YOUR TREE
> OR STEAL YOUR IDEA
> ISN'T ABOUT TO TAKE
> YOUR LITTLE ACT OF
> REVENGE LYING DOWN.

** Or woman, of course.

# RULE 43

## Look After Yourself

You are the Boss, the Captain, the Driving Force. If you are sick, who is going to run the ship? There is no one else. It makes sense to look after yourself. And I have no intention of getting all preachy here and telling you to go to bed early, eat your greens, and do loads of exercise—that would all be pure hypocrisy because I don't do any of those things. Doesn't mean *you* shouldn't, however. They are all a good idea.

An occasional quick body service might be a good idea, a regular check-up to nip any potential problems in the bud. I have an annual one. I would also suggest that some foods are like dynamite and they fill you with energy, speed your metabolism, and make you feel great. Other foods make you sluggish, get stored as fat, and slow you down. They might also do you long-term damage in the way of clogging up your arteries. Now the choice is entirely yours, but the machine that is you runs better on high-energy food and worse on junk food.

Same with sleep. Going without makes you tired. Having too much makes you lethargic. Getting the right amount makes you feel good. Going back to sleep makes you feel blurry. Getting up straight away makes you feel good—and noble. Nothing better. But, of course, all this is entirely up to you. No one is going to stand behind you anymore and make sure you've washed behind your ears or check that your shoes are clean and polished. You're a grown-up and on your own now. Fantastic. But it means you have all the responsibility, too.

Rules Players eat well, sleep well, relax a lot, exercise. (And no, computer games don't count.) They also stay away from potentially harmful situations. They know how to say out of danger, avoid threatening encounters, and generally take care of themselves.

Looking after yourself is exactly that. Not relying on anyone else to make sure you are fed on time and fed well, washed and ready to go, comfortable, tidy, healthy, and let out regularly for your walk. It's great being a grown-up. You get to stay up all night partying if you want to, but you can also choose to take care of yourself if you want to.

YOU'RE A GROWN-UP
AND
ON YOUR OWN NOW.

# RULE 44

# Maintain Good Manners in All Things

In her wonderful book Watching the English,* Kate Fox observes that in any small transaction, like buying a newspaper, there will be around three pleases and two thank-yous—and that's a minimum. We have to interact with a whole host of people every day, and a little politeness has to be a good thing. The Rules Player maintains good manners in all things. And if you don't know what good manners are, then we are in trouble.

You're probably thinking that you have good manners already. Most of us believe we do. However, the more you hurry and the more stress you are under, the more manners are likely to slip. All of us, if we're honest, will admit to forgetting to properly express gratitude for something when frazzled by life or feeling a huge temptation to push in front of somebody old when rushing to catch a bus.

However rushed and fraught you are (and following the Rules should make you less so), you should always make the effort to show these good manners:

- Lining up without pushing
- Complimenting people when you need to (and when they deserve it—no use throwing compliments around if they aren't justified and earned)
- Not sticking your nose in where it isn't wanted

---

* *Watching the English: The Hidden Rules of English Behaviour* by Kate Fox (Hodder & Stoughton, 2004).

- Keeping a promise
- Keeping a secret
- Keeping basic table etiquette (oh, come on, you know this stuff: no elbows, no talking with your mouth open, no overstuffing your mouth, no flicking peas with your knife)
- Not shouting at people who get in your way
- Apologizing when you get in someone else's
- Being civil
- Not swearing or being religiously profane
- Opening the door ahead of people
- Standing back when there's a rush
- Answering when spoken to
- Saying "good morning"
- Thanking people when they've looked after you or done something for you
- Being hospitable
- Observing manners of other communities
- Not grabbing the last piece of cake
- Being courteous and charming
- Offering visitors refreshment and going to the front door to say goodbye to them

No matter how many small interactions with people you have each day, don't let the manners slip. They cost nothing and yet can generate so much goodwill and make everyone's life that much more pleasant.

# RULE 45

# Prune Your Stuff Frequently

Why? Because collecting clutter clutters your home, your life, and your mind. A cluttered home is symbolic of cluttered thinking. Rules Players are clear and direct in their thinking and don't collect junk. If only. We all do, of course. All I am suggesting is that occasionally clearing some of it out might be a good idea, or it overwhelms you emotionally and gets more and more cobwebby.

Pruning your stuff gives you a chance to get rid of anything that is useless, broken, out of date, uncool, uncleanable, redundant, and ugly. It was, after all, William Morris who said not to have anything in your home that wasn't useful or beautiful. Having a good clear-out refreshes you, revitalizes you, makes you conscious of what you are collecting—and anything that makes us conscious is a good thing in my book.

Again, I have noticed a difference between successful people and those who seem to labor in a backwater never really getting their lives off the ground. Those who are punchy and getting on with things are also those who have an amazing ability to prune stuff, clear the clutter, sort the wheat from the chaff. Those who are having trouble getting lift-off are those running along the tarmac still clutching black plastic sacks full of useless stuff they bought from the charity shop and have never thrown away—or opened since they bought them, cupboards full of junk that is just taking up space, drawers full of broken things, and closets full of clothes they can no longer get into or which have so long gone out of fashion they may be worth something as collector's items but will never be worn again.

There is an "unburdening" effect that comes with pruning. You have more space in your home, you have a feeling of being more in control, and you get rid of that slightly overwhelmed feeling that comes with having piles of stuff accumulating everywhere. You don't have to live in a spotless house full of designer furniture and minimalist styling. All I'm suggesting is that if you want to find out what's holding you back, try looking in the cabinet under the sink or under the bed or on the top shelf of the closet in the spare room.

CLUTTER OVERWHELMS YOU EMOTIONALLY AND GETS MORE AND MORE COBWEBBY.

# RULE 46

## Remember to Touch Base

Before you can touch base, you have to know where base is. Base is home. Base is where you belong. Base is where you feel comfortable, secure, loved, restored, and trusted. Base is where you feel strong and in control. Base is anywhere you can kick your shoes off, metaphorically and physically, and rest your head safe in the knowledge you'll be looked after.

We all lead increasingly busy, frenetic, and frantic lives. We all get caught up in the busyness of life to such an extent that we lose sight of where we thought we were going and what we thought we were going to do and what we were going to achieve. Base is going back to where you dreamed it all, planned it all out. Base is where you were before you got lost.

Base camp might well be rediscovering our roots—essential in an age when we all move around so much. Knowing who your family is, where you come from, what your real background is. It's OK to have ambition and move on from our roots, but it's also important to know who we are and where we came from. You can sometimes sense it in celebrities who have become incredibly famous or rich. Often they try to deny their past and pretend to be something else; in the process they come across as shallow and fake.

For you, base might be a place where you grew up, where you're reminded of the feelings of growing up—the hopes and fears, the younger you. Or it might be a person who provides the base—a best friend from many years ago who can remind you of how you were before it all got so confusing.

Of course, we might not all know where we came from, and we have to make allowances for that. You might be adopted, but you were raised somewhere. Whatever your circumstances, you will have something that makes you feel grounded if you look for it. It doesn't have to be where you were born and raised. If you are really struggling, then it's possible to create yourself a new base. Anywhere that makes you feel secure is fine.

We all need time with people or in places where we can be ourselves, where we don't have to explain, justify, provide background or give a good impression. That's the joy of touching base—being somewhere you are accepted without question and everything around you reminds you of what's really important. Touching base is something that, when we do it, we wonder why on earth we left it so long.

BASE IS WHERE YOU WERE
BEFORE YOU GOT LOST.

# RULE 47

# Draw the Lines Around Yourself

Personal boundaries are the imaginary lines you draw around yourself that no one should cross either physically—unless invited in—or emotionally. You are entitled to respect, privacy, decency, kindness, love, truth, and honor, to name but a few rights. If people cross the lines, blur the boundaries, you are entitled to stand up for yourself and say, "No, I won't put up with this."

But you have to draw the lines first. You have to know what you will stand for and what you won't. You have to set the boundaries in your own mind before you can expect others to respect them, stick to them.

The more secure you become with your boundaries, the less power other people will have to affect you. The more clearly defined your boundaries, the more you realize that other people's stuff is more to do with them and less to do with you—you stop taking things so personally.

You are entitled to basic self-respect. You can't expect others to respect you unless you respect yourself. You can't respect yourself until you have formed a clear picture of who you are and what you are. And setting boundaries is part of this process. You have to feel important enough to set those lines. And once set, you have to be assertive enough to reinforce them.

Setting personal boundaries means you don't have to be scared of other people anymore. You now have a clear idea of what you will put up with and what you won't. Once someone crosses the line between appropriate and inappropriate behavior, it gets really easy to say, "No, I don't want to be treated like this/spoken to like this."

Probably the best way to start this is with your own family. Over the years, we get set in patterns of behavior. Say, for example, you might be used to going to visit your parents and coming away feeling bad because they put you down or made you feel inadequate. You can change things by saying to yourself, "I won't put up with this anymore." And then don't put up with it. Speak your mind. Say you don't like being criticized/told off/made to feel small; you are an adult now and are entitled to respect and encouragement. Setting personal boundaries enables us to resist pushy people, rude people, aggressive people, people who would take advantage of us, people who would use us unwisely and unwell. Successful people know their worth and don't get messed around. Successful people are the ones who can recognize emotional blackmail, people playing games with them, people on the make, people who themselves are weak and needy, people who dump on others, people who need to make you look small to make themselves feel big. Once you've got those lines drawn around you, it gets a whole lot easier to stay behind them and be firm, resolute, strong, and assertive.

SETTING PERSONAL BOUNDARIES MEANS YOU DON'T HAVE TO BE SCARED OF OTHER PEOPLE ANYMORE.

# Shop for Quality, Not Price

I have to admit my wife taught me this one, for which I am eternally in her debt. To me it seemed a natural thing to shop for price. Perhaps this is what men do. I would work out what I wanted and then go and buy the cheapest items I could and feel really pleased with myself for saving money. And then I was always dissatisfied with what I had. Stuff broke or didn't work or wore out quickly or looked shoddy after a very short time. I was living in a mess—and a cheap one at that. What I needed to learn was the art of quality shopping.

Basically:

- Accept only the very best—second best is not for you, ever.
- If you can't afford it, don't buy it or wait and save until you can.
- If you have to have it, buy the very best you can afford.

There, that's pretty easy, isn't it? Well, for me it wasn't as easy as that. It took me quite a long time to really get to grips with this one. It isn't that I don't—or didn't then—admire quality or appreciate excellence; it was that I was impulsive. If I thought I needed something, I wanted it right then and there. And if I couldn't afford the very best, I would settle for the cheapest. In fact, in a very English sort of way, I thought that "getting a bargain" was what it was all about. We don't like to talk about money, and we don't like to brag about how much something cost, too tacky by far—better to buy tacky in the first place. I think not.

Going for quality doesn't mean we're stuck up or living beyond our means—if you can't afford it, don't buy it. Going for quality means you appreciate the finer things, can see the sense in buying well-made, well-produced things because they will:

- Last longer
- Be stronger
- Not break so easily

And this means they will not need to be replaced so often, which means you might actually be saving money. They will also make you look and feel better.

Now that I've latched on to this Rule, I really enjoy that anticipation before I buy something. I make sure it really is the quality I am going for and not just the price. I still shop around for a bargain, though—it's just now I look for the quality items but I'm prepared to find them at the lowest price.

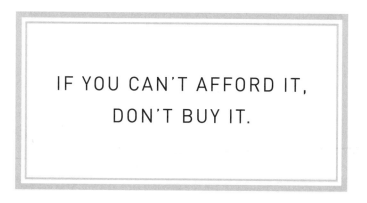

IF YOU CAN'T AFFORD IT,
DON'T BUY IT.

# RULE 49

## It's OK to Worry, or to Know How Not To

The future is uncertain, scary, hidden. We wouldn't be human if we didn't worry about things at times. We worry about our health, our parents/kids/friends, our relationships, our work, and our spending. We worry that we are getting older, fatter, poorer, more tired, less attractive, less fit, less mentally alert, less everything really. We worry about things that matter and things that don't. Sometimes we worry about not worrying.

Look, it really is OK to worry—just so long as there is something real to worry about. If there isn't, then all you're doing is putting wrinkles in your brow—and that makes you look older, you know.

The first step is to decide whether there is something you can do about whatever it is you are worrying about, or not. There are usually logical steps to take to eliminate that worry. I worry that people aren't taking those steps, which means they are choosing to hang on to their worries rather than be free of them.

If you are worried then:

- Get practical advice
- Get up-to-date information
- Do something, anything as long as it is constructive

If you are worrying about your health, go and see a doctor. If you are worrying about money, set a budget and spend wisely. If you are worrying about your weight, go to the gym—eat less, do more. If you are worrying about a lost kitten, phone the vet/police/local animal rescue. If you are worrying about getting older, there is simply no point—it's happening whether you worry or not.

If there is nothing you can do about your worry (or if you are a persistent worrier, even bordering on the neurotic), then distraction is the only answer. Get absorbed in something else. A man with the rather impressive name of Mikhail Csikszentmihalyi identified something called "flow," where you are so absorbed in a task you are doing, so fully immersed, that you become almost unaware of external events. It's a pleasurable experience, and it completely banishes worry. He also said, "The quality of our lives improves immensely when there is at least one other person who is willing to listen to our troubles."

Worrying may be a symptom that you don't really want to do something about the problem. It might be easier just to carry on worrying—or looking concerned and appearing to worry—rather than doing something about it. It is OK to worry properly, profitably, usefully. It is not OK to worry pointlessly or needlessly. Or at least, it is OK, but it's a colossal waste of life.

---

...ALL YOU'RE DOING IS PUTTING WRINKLES IN YOUR BROW—AND THAT MAKES YOU LOOK OLDER, YOU KNOW.

# Stay Young

I did say earlier that if you were worrying about getting older, you should stop because there wasn't anything you could do about it. It's inevitable. So why a Rule saying Stay young? Well, growing older physically (and temporally) is something we all have to do, and putting it off by endless surgery and the like is pointless. Better to stay young. And by this I mean mentally and emotionally. Billy Connolly made a wry observation in one of his shows when he bent down to pick something up and made a noise, a sort of bending grunt that oldies make. And he said he didn't know when he had started to make that noise, but it had crept up on him and he made it now. That's what I'm talking about—all those noises and actions we make to indicate we're old. All that wrapping up well when we go out in case we catch a cold. All that making sure we take our coat off when we come in, even if we're going straight out again, or we won't feel the benefit. All that, "I'd rather just have a cup of coffee if it's all right with you" stuff. All that "We're going to the same place we always go on vacation— you know what you're getting."

I was reading yesterday about a man who had just taken his father backpacking in the Greek islands. His dad is aged 78 and he said he had trouble keeping up with him. Now that's staying young. I know a woman in her sixties who describes how she feels the same inside now as she did when she was 21. And it shows outside. That's staying young.

Staying young is trying new things, not grumbling or saying all the things you know people say as they get older. It's not going for the safe option; it's staying abreast of what is happening, not giving up stuff like cycling because you think you're too old for it. (If you are very young, by the way, I do apologize for all this, but you will need it one day, believe me.)

Staying young is trying out new tastes, new places to go, new styles, keeping an open mind, not getting reactionary (hmmm, I should read this again) or being disapproving of more and more things, not settling for what you've always had or always done. Staying young is about keeping a fresh vision of the world, being interested, being stimulated, being motivated, being adventurous.

Staying young is a state of mind.

STAYING YOUNG IS
TRYING OUT NEW TASTES,
NEW PLACES TO GO,
NEW STYLES.

# RULE 51

# Throwing Money at a Problem Doesn't Always Work

Years ago when I worked in one particular industry, whenever something was going wrong, my boss would always sigh and suggest throwing money at the problem until it went away. At work this approach often works wonders, but problems in life tend to need a more hands-on approach, a more delicate touch. We tend to think that if we just chuck enough money at things they'll get sorted out, instead of finding ways to really sort them out that require time and attention and care.

Let's go back to that getting older thing again. You might think that throwing money at it in the shape of cosmetic surgery might be the answer but it isn't; it only delays things and can create worse problems than it solves. How much better to work on one's mental approach to aging and come to terms with it in a dignified and graceful way instead. If somebody you care about seems distracted, tense, not themselves, then buying them a present might well cheer them up, but the better (and cheaper) option is to make time to take them out for a walk and ask them about themselves, give them the opportunity to talk.

We tend to think that if we spend more money on something, it will solve the problem. Maybe sometimes we need an old-fashioned approach of time and attention and finding out. Like our grandparents, who didn't throw things away and get a new one when something had stopped working—they patiently sat down and tried to sort out what it was that had gone wrong and determine if there was a way to put it right again. That went for relationships as well as for watches or appliances.

Throwing money at things makes us feel powerful and grown-up when instead we might need to stand back and see if we couldn't do better by changing the situation another way. I know I'm as guilty of this one as anybody. It happens to me most with cars. I buy a car—usually an expensive, temperamental, costly to fix model. Then when something goes wrong, as it invariably does, I pay the garage to tow it away and spend a fortune having it repaired. How much simpler my life would be if I could stand back and see that the car was unsuitable in the first place, basically a mistake. Throwing money at it now doesn't alleviate the problem; it merely delays it, puts it off until the next time when it goes wrong again. And it will. Oh, believe me, it will; it always does.

THROWING MONEY AT
IT NOW DOESN'T
ALLEVIATE THE PROBLEM;
IT MERELY DELAYS IT.

# Think for Yourself

You'll think this one's so obvious you'll be wondering what it's doing in here, and I do apologize if it seems patronizing, simplistic, or downright rude. I don't mean to offend or insult, and I do appreciate that you do think for yourself. I guess what I mean by this Rule is that we need to be incredibly clear about our opinions, grounded in our own sense of identity, and very assertive about being us so that we aren't easily swayed by what other people think of us. It's tougher than it looks at first glance. We are all vulnerable inside. We all have fears and concerns. We all want to be loved and accepted. We all want to blend in, be one of a crowd, be acknowledged. We all want to belong. The temptation is to say, "I'll be whatever you want me to be."

Being original or creative or different can make us think we stand out too much and will get shunned. But truly successful people aren't shunned; they instead become pack leader because of their originality, their difference. If you are obnoxious or rude or hurtful, you will indeed be shunned. But if you are kind, thoughtful, caring, and respectful you will be loved and accepted. If you are also original in your thinking, you will be looked up to, respected, and admired.

To think for yourself, you have to be pretty sure of who you are and be clear in your thinking as well as doing it for yourself—there's no point in thinking for yourself if it's all muddled and woolly.

I have a friend who is very intelligent and astute, but all her opinions come from reading a particular national newspaper.

Whatever line it takes on a particular issue is the same line she will come out with. She trusts her paper implicitly and is unable to see how predictable her views are—seeing as they are always based on what she has read. She will argue her case articulately, forcefully, and in a well reasoned way, but always absolutely in line with her paper's views. We can all be a bit like that and need to change where we get our information from occasionally to make sure we stay fresh and original.

Of course, to think for yourself means you have to (a) have something to think about and (b) actually do the thinking. Look at a selection of people you know. If they are at one with their own life, I bet they are doing both. If they are badly adjusted and generally struggling, I bet they're not doing either.

WE ALL WANT TO
BLEND IN,
BE ONE OF A CROWD,
BE ACKNOWLEDGED.
WE ALL WANT TO BELONG.

# You Are Not in Charge

Sorry if this comes as a shock, but you're not in charge, no matter how much you want to be, no matter how much you think you are, no matter how much you deserve to be. If you are not in charge, it doesn't mean anybody else is either. We may all be on the same runaway train with no driver or there may indeed be a driver. (The driver may be insane, drunk, or asleep, but that's another thing entirely.)

Once you accept that you're not in charge, you can let go of so much stuff it's very liberating. Instead of complaining, "Why isn't it like this?" you can accept it isn't and let it go. Instead of metaphorically bashing your head against a metaphoric brick wall, you can walk away whistling with your hands in your pockets—you are, after all, not in charge and therefore not responsible.

Once you get your head around the wonderful concept that you are here to enjoy and not here to run things, then you are free to sit in the sunshine a bit more often, take time off.

Look, stuff happens. Good stuff and bad stuff. There may or there may not be a driver. You can blame the driver if you want. You can accept that if there isn't a driver, the journey will sometimes be scary, sometimes exhilarating, sometimes boring, sometimes beautiful. (Actually, whether there is or isn't a driver, the same holds true.) We have to have both the good stuff and the bad stuff. That's a fact. If you or I were in charge, we'd probably interfere too much and get rid of most of the bad stuff and the human race would die out ever so quickly due to stagnation, lack of challenge,  lack of motivation, and lack of excitement. It is, after all, the bad stuff that fires us up, makes us learn, and gives us a reason for living. If it was all good, it would be awfully fluffy and boring.

A slight condition to this one, though. You might not be running the show, but that doesn't discharge you of all responsibilities. You still have obligations—you still need to be respectful of the world you live in and the people you live in it with—it's just that you don't have overall responsibility for the whole show and everything in it.

Seeing as you are not in charge, you can watch it like a movie and cheer at the exciting bits, cry at the sad bits, and hide during the scary moments. But you are not the director or even the projectionist. You are not even the usher.* You are the audience; enjoy the show.

> ## ONCE YOU ACCEPT THAT YOU'RE NOT IN CHARGE, YOU CAN LET GO.

* There's probably a frightfully modern PC word for this job. Please don't write in.

# RULE 54

# Have Something in Your Life That Takes You Out of Yourself

I have a friend who swears by her adopted greyhounds. No, I don't mean she stands next to them and curses, although I'm sure she does from time to time. But what I mean is that no matter how miserable she is, no matter how hard she's been working, no matter how annoying life has been, no matter how fed up, cross, or what sort of a bad hair day she's had, when she gets home and gets that incredible greeting from her rescued dogs, it all then becomes worthwhile. The gloom is lifted, and she is instantly restored, calm, happy, and loved. It's a bit sad, but there you go (only joking).

For me, it has to be my children and where I live. Although my kids drive me insane at times, there is still something incredibly magical about the way they view the world and how they grow. As for where I live, I only have to think about going home to feel lifted and invigorated.

For every one of us, there will be something different that does it, that pushes our button in a very positive way. And I find the wonderful thing about this Rule is that it invariably isn't the things that cost money that have this power. The things that lift us are usually magical in some way—a particular view or person, a pet or a child, a favorite book or film that we turn to, to help us recharge. It might be a state of mind that we arrive at through some ritual such as going to a place of worship or meditating. It might be a certain piece of music that lightens our heart. For some it will be reorganizing their stamp collection; for others it will be doing charity work or being a volunteer. (There's nothing like doing something for others or for a greater good to take you out of yourself.)

# RULE 54

Whatever it is, make sure you have it, know it and use it. What's the good of a piece of music that always lifts your mood if you don't play it occasionally?

I guess we all need something in our life that takes us out of ourselves and perhaps stops us taking ourselves too seriously. Whether it's a dog, a child, or a chat with a lonely person in a nursing home, there needs to be something that makes you realize that all the stuff that's getting to you isn't that important and reminds you of the simple pleasures in life.

> WHAT'S THE GOOD OF A
> PIECE OF MUSIC THAT
> ALWAYS LIFTS YOUR MOOD
> IF YOU DON'T PLAY IT
> OCCASIONALLY?

# Only the Good Feel Guilty

Bad people don't feel guilty. They are too busy being bad. Good people feel guilty because they are good and they feel they have done wrong, let somebody down, made a mistake, or screwed up somewhere. Good people have a conscience. Bad people don't. If you do feel guilty, that's a good sign. It shows you are on the right track. But you have to know how to deal with it, because guilt is a terribly selfish emotion. It is wasteful and pointless.

We have two choices: put it right or dump the guilt. Yes, we all make mistakes. We all screw up from time to time. We don't always do "the right thing." And if we've got a con-science, we will feel guilty sometimes. But guilt is utterly pointless unless it is acted on for the better. You would be better off feeling something else* if you aren't going to act on your guilt.

If you hang around feeling guilty but don't do anything about it, then it's a waste of time and life.

The first thing to do is to assess whether you really need to feel guilty. It could just be an overdeveloped conscience or sense of duty. If you are the kind of person always to volun-teer, but just this once you say "no," then there is no need to feel guilty. You'll know deep down if you've earned this one off. If you've a choice between doing something or not, then it's simple: do it or don't do it but without guilt. Make the

---

* Self loathing, fear, panic—all good substitutes for guilt if you really must. But better just to let it go.

choice with that in mind. Not doing it and feeling guilty is not an option.

If you do have cause to feel guilty, then if you can, put it right. That's the simplest course of action. And what if you can't put things right? Then learn the lesson, make a resolution, dump the guilt, and move on. If it keeps on gnawing away at you, you have to find a way to put it behind you.

IF YOU DO FEEL GUILTY,
THAT'S A GOOD SIGN.

# If You Can't Say Anything Nice, Don't Say Anything at All

It is very easy to moan, to complain, to criticize. It is much harder to always find something nice to say about a situation or a person. But think of it now as a huge challenge. Saying something nice is hard because our natural inclination is to moan. If someone asks how the weekend camping went, it's easier to start on the bad weather and the problems with the campsite and the annoying behavior of the people in the next-door trailer, than it is the joy of being with people you wanted to be with and in a fantastic setting. When a friend asks how you're getting on with your boss, the things they do that really annoy you usually spring to mind before the upsides.

No matter how horrid someone is, there is always something about him that is good. Your job is to find that good bit and highlight it, speak about it, draw attention to it. Same with a situation that seems troublesome. I remember reading once of someone who was on the Metro in Paris during a major strike. It was chaos, and people were shoving and pushing. It was pretty horrendous. There was a woman with a small child there, and it could have been quite scary. She bent down to the child and said quite brightly, "This, my dear, is what they call an adventure." It has become a pet phrase of mine in times of crisis and trouble.

When asked your opinion of someone, something, some-where, you need to find something good to say, something flattering and positive. There is ample evidence that being positive has many benefits, but the most noticeable is that people will gravitate toward you and not even know why. That positive air about you is attractive. People like being around those who are upbeat, positive, happy, and confident. We need to bite our tongue more and say good things more often.

Obviously, if you are only going to say good things, then this cuts out back-biting, gossiping, mouthing off, telling tales, being rude about people, and complaining (you are allowed to point out defects or problems but in a constructive way). And that could leave you with a big gap to fill.

Before opening your mouth, try—just for a week—to find something good to say. It's one of those things that will amaze you by how it improves your life, but don't take my word for it—just try it. And if all else fails, and you really can't think of anything positive to say at all, then don't say anything. At all.

THIS, MY DEAR,
IS WHAT THEY CALL
AN ADVENTURE.

# PART II

# PARTNERSHIP
# RULES

We all need to love and to be loved. Most of us want the comfort of a relationship and the closeness of companionship that such a relationship brings. We aren't islands, and we do need to share together with someone very dear and close to us. 'Tis human nature. We wouldn't be the fantastic people we are without that need to give and to be given to.

But, and this is a big but (does my but look big in this?), human relationships being what they are, this is an enormous area in which to make mistakes, fall flat on our face, and generally make a dog's dinner out of the whole business. We need Rules here like they are going out of style. We need all the guidance we can get. Right, that's enough about me.

But seriously, we do all need help, and sometimes it pays to come at the subject from a slightly different angle. What follows are some unusual Rules to get you thinking about your relationship from a new perspective.

None of this is revolutionary, but these are the Rules I've noticed those who have successful, productive, sustaining, long-lasting, and nurturing relationships have about them. They are also the ones having exciting, stimulating, extremely close, and powerful relationships.

# RULE 57

## Accept the Differences, Embrace What You Have in Common

*"Sugar and spice and all things nice...slugs and snails and puppy dogs' tails"*—isn't that how the rhyme goes? So which are you? The slugs and snails or the sugar and spice? Chances are, you're a bit of both. Look, it's true that men and women have differences. We would be fools if we didn't accept and recognize that. But we're not so different that we are separate species—or from separate planets, as some would have us believe. We actually have more in common than we have different. If we embrace those things we have in common and accept what is different, we might get along a whole lot better instead of treating each other as if we were separate species.

A relationship is, if you like, a team made up of initially two people (later the team may get swamped by lots of junior team members) who both bring talents and skills and resources to the relationship. Every team needs different people with different qualities to achieve things and to make the project work. If you are both strong leaders, quick decision makers, and impulsive hotheads, then who is going to see to the detail and finish off projects? Who is going to do the work instead of just generating the ideas? Never mind just accepting the differences—see the benefits! Try to view differences in the light of them being special talents—differences that could be used effectively to make your team function better.

And what of the things you have in common? Those can be great (shared views, shared tastes), but they don't always make life simple (shared love of being right, shared need to be in control). If you are both genuine leaders, you might both be wrestling for the driver's seat. Instead, agree to take turns leading. The things in common should be celebrated and used—in combination or alternately—to really fire you both up and make the relationship special and successful.

Look, you're in this together—whatever "this" is—and you need to work together to make it successful. If you combine the talents you have in common, you will get a lot further and have an easier time of it than if you both pull in different directions. Strip away the layers, and we are all human, all frightened, all vulnerable, all trying to make some sort of sense out of our lives. If we focus on the differences and make a big deal out of them, we risk losing the input and contribution of somebody who can help to lighten our load and make the journey more fun. All those crass Internet jokes—if a woman was a computer she would be this, and if a man was a car he'd be that—really don't help. Real life isn't like that.

> WE MIGHT GET ALONG A WHOLE LOT BETTER INSTEAD OF TREATING EACH OTHER AS IF WE WERE SEPARATE SPECIES.

# RULE 58

## Allow* Your Partner the Space to Be Themselves

It's a funny old thing, but we often fall in love with someone who is independent, forceful, powerful, in charge, in control, and very much out in the world. Then, the second we've captured this person, so to speak, we try to change her. We come over all jealous if our partner carries on being as independent; as if being in a relationship with us somehow limits her, ties her down, cuts her wings off.

Before we met our partner, she managed quite well without us. The second we meet her, we start giving her advice, restricting her choices, limiting her vision and dreams, curtailing her freedom. We need to stand back and give her the freedom to be herself.

A lot of people say that the magic of their relationship has worn off, that there is no sparkle there any more and that they have grown apart. And then when you look into it a bit more deeply, you find two people locked in a symbiotic relationship of mistrust, oppression, and petty encroachment. They don't give each other any space at all, let alone space to be themselves.

So what can we do? First, stand back and see your partner as she was when you first met her. What attracted you? What was special about them? What turned you on?

Now look at your partner. What is different? What has gone and what has been replaced? Is she still the same independent person, or have you eroded her space, confidence, independence, vitality? Maybe not, that seems a bit harsh, but

*Yes, yes, I know I said "'Allow." It is a joke, don't write in…

unconsciously we do tend to rein our partners in a bit, and they do lose their sparkle.

You have to encourage your partner to step outside of the coziness of the relationship and rediscover her energy and vitality. She may need to spend some time rediscovering her talents and skills at independence. And you may need to sit on your hands at times to avoid reining her in again. So encourage, stand back, sit on your hands, push, and be there. Tall order. Most successful relationships have an element, and a big one, of independence. The couple spends time apart to bring something back to the relationship. This is healthy. This is good. This is grown-up.

> WHAT ATTRACTED YOU?
> WHAT WAS
> SPECIAL ABOUT HER?
> WHAT TURNED YOU ON?

# RULE 59

## Be Nice

It is very easy in the busyness of modern life and the complex sparring of a day-to-day relationship to forget that we are dealing with a real live human being here and not just someone we bounce off as we go along. It is easy to start to take people for granted, to think we've thanked them or praised them or said "please," when instead we ignored them, were rude by the guilty sin of omission, disregarded them, and generally behaved like they were pond life by default.

To make the relationship go with a zing, you have to go back to square one and start being courteous again in the old-fashioned sense of the word. You have to reintroduce yourselves to each other as respectful, tactful individuals who are going to start again being pleasant, kind, civil, and polite. From now on, you will say "please" and "thank you" no matter how many times a day it is necessary. Be thoughtful. Be complimentary. Give gifts without there being any reason for it. Ask questions to show you are interested in what your partner is saying.

Be solicitous of your partner's health, welfare, dreams, hopes, workload, interests, and pleasure. Take time to help him. Take time to focus on his needs and wants. Take time to just be there for him, not to have to do anything except listen, show an interest, show that you still love him. Don't allow benign neglect to ruin your relationship.

We treat strangers exceedingly well and usually reserve our best attentions for people we work with. Our partner gets missed, lost in the bustle of it all. In fact, we should treat our partner better than anyone else. After all, this is supposed to be the most important person in the world to us. It makes sense to show him this is true.

Of course, if you already do all this, you must excuse me reminding you to.

I was reading about a man who kept buying his wife new handbags—always unsuitable ones, not big enough or tough enough for her needs. She tried explaining that she was quite happy to buy her own bags as she was a grown-up, but he had gotten it into his head that his idea of "style" was so much better than hers. In the end she bought him a bag, and that shut him up for a bit. I thought this a wonderfully Zen solution. She didn't get cross or yell at him, but just gently poked fun at him. Brilliant.

> GO BACK TO
> SQUARE ONE AND
> START BEING
> COURTEOUS AGAIN.

# RULE 60

## You Want to Do What?

Just because we come together to be a couple for however long doesn't mean we are joined at the hip and have to think the same, do the same, feel the same, react the same. I have noticed that the most successful relationships are the ones where the couple is strong together but also strong apart. The best relationships are the ones where both are supportive of each other's interests even if they aren't their own.

Being supportive of your partner and what she wants to do means you have to be very centered yourself not to feel jealous or mistrustful or resentful. You have to be prepared for her to be independent, strong, out in the world separate from you. It can be hard. It can ask a lot of you. It can be a real test of how much you care and how protective you tend to be.

The more freedom you give/allow/tolerate/encourage, the more likely your partner will be to reciprocate and return. If a partner feels she is encouraged and trusted, she is much less likely to "stray" or want out because she feels hemmed in or caged. The more supportive you are, the more she will feel she is being treated kindly, and that is a good thing.

But what if you disagree with what your partner wants to do? Then you have to look at your own stuff, I'm afraid. You see, your partner is a separate human being and entitled to do pretty well whatever she wants to do—assuming it isn't hurtful to you or in any serious way jeopardizes the relationship (such as sleeping with other people or committing crimes)— and it is your role to be supportive. You may need to question what it is about what she wants to do that you find hard to go along with. This might be more about you than your partner.

Ask yourself—if she does this, if she goes ahead, what's the worst that can happen? She makes a mess of your floor, ruins part of the garden, spends money on something you don't really want, isn't around much for a week. Now compare that to the thought of her leaving or living with you frustrated and unhappy. Which is worse?

Of course, just because your partner says she wants to do something doesn't mean she will. Some very stubborn types will, however, be more likely to go ahead and do it just because you're objecting to everything they mention. Say "yes" and they might well never bother anyway.

If you look ahead to Rule 64, you will read about how you should treat your partner better than your best friend, and being supportive is part of this. We forget that our partner is a separate entity. We forget that our partner, too, has dreams and plans and unfulfilled ambitions. It is our job to encourage our partner to find their path, to realize those ambitions, to stretch herself to her fullest extent, to be complete and satisfied and fulfilled. It is not our job to put her down, ridicule her dreams, belittle her plans, or laugh at her ambitions. It is not our job to discourage her, put her off, place obstacles in her path, or restrict her in any way. It is our job to encourage our partner to soar.

YOU HAVE TO BE PREPARED
FOR HER TO BE
INDEPENDENT, STRONG,
OUT IN THE WORLD
SEPARATE FROM YOU.

# RULE 61

## Be the First to Say Sorry

Don't care who started it. Don't care what it was about. Don't care who is right and who is wrong. Don't care whose game it was. You are both behaving like spoiled brats and should go to your room at once. No seriously, we all fall out from time to time; that's human nature. From now on, if you want to be a committed Rules Player, and I can see from the glint in your eye you do, you will be the first to say sorry. That's it. End of Rule. Why? Because that's what Rules Players do. We are the first. We take great pride in being first because we are so firm in our own sense of ourselves that we don't feel any loss of pride if we say sorry. We don't feel threatened or challenged or weak. We can say sorry and still be strong. We can say sorry and retain our dignity and respect.

We will say sorry because we are sorry. We are sorry to have become embroiled in an argument of any sort and have by the very nature of arguing forgotten at least five Rules.

You see, if it has gotten as far as a falling out, no matter how trivial or minor, we have already committed a few cardinal mistakes and thus should be the first to say sorry because we are in the wrong no matter what the argument is about. Arguing is what we are saying sorry for. Never mind what it was about; we are saying sorry first because we are noble, kind, generous in spirit, dignified, mature, sensible, and good. I know, I know, gosh we have to be all these things and still say sorry. Tough call, tall order. Just do it, and see how good it makes you feel. The view is always fantastic from the moral high ground.

# RULE 61

And what if you are both reading this book? Heavens. Then you must not tell each other you are—Rule 1—but then race to be the first to say sorry. Could be interesting. Let me know how you get on.

Saying sorry has many benefits, even if it does stick in your throat a little. Not only does it give you the moral advantage, but it also diffuses tension, gets rid of bad feelings, and clears the air. Chances are that if you say sorry first, your partner will probably be humbled into apologizing also. Maybe.

Always remember you are not apologizing for the sin or crime or faux pas you have committed—you are apologizing for being so immature to have argued in the first place, apologizing for losing your cool, apologizing for forgetting Rules, apologizing for being boorish or argumentative or stubborn or rude or childish or whatever. You can come out of your room now.

> WE CAN SAY SORRY AND
> RETAIN OUR DIGNITY AND
> RESPECT.

# RULE 62

## Go That Extra Step in Trying to Please Them

What? You have to be the first to say you are sorry, encourage and support them, give them freedom, be supportive, be nice, and now I am saying go that extra step in trying to please them as well. Heck, anyone would think you were doing this out of love. You'd think this was for someone you adored and worshipped and respected and had great affection for—someone you really cared about. Precisely. That is exactly what it's about. This is about going an extra step to please the person who means the most to you in all the world, the person you love and cherish and care about, the person who is the most important human being in your life. This is about your love, your companion, your treasure, your soul mate, your lover, and friend. So what's your problem? Why wouldn't you want to do this? Why wouldn't you be doing it already?

So if we want to, what is it we are supposed to be doing? Easy: thinking ahead. Planning birthdays that are more than just a present, a card, some flowers, and a couple of drinks at the bar—and that's if they're lucky this year. It's thinking about what they would like, what they might want, for birthdays, special treats, days off, long weekends, and anniversaries. It's thinking of extravagances, luxuries, indulgences. It's going out of your way to find out what they would really, really like and then giving it to them. And I'm not talking money here. This is about surprising them, finding little things to delight them and show that you have thought of them. Arranging things in advance to let them know how special they are and how much you care and how important they are.

# RULE 62

This is finding ways to delight them beyond the normal, way beyond what is expected, further than anyone else would. This is a fantastic opportunity to be creative, adventurous, wacky, unusual, caring, and loving all at the same time. Haven't got the time? Then you must check your priority list. What could be more important than delighting your lover and partner and friend? (Yes, it is the same person, not three people.)

> ## WHY WOULDN'T YOU WANT TO DO THIS? WHY WOULDN'T YOU BE DOING IT ALREADY?

# RULE 63

## Always Have Someone—or Something—That Is Pleased to See You

We're back to the woman and her greyhounds here. When she comes home, her dogs are always pleased to see her, but then dogs always are. No matter how badly you have treated them,* they always go nuts. Of course, you want your partner to behave in just the same fashion, to go nuts when you come home. And I'm sure they do, don't they? And, of course, you do when they come home, don't you? No? Why not? Yes? Well done.

We all need someone who is pleased to see us. It makes us feel it is all worthwhile. I love it when I have to go away for work for a day or two and then when I get back my children all stand there, like children do, with their hands outstretched with that lovely, "Have you brought me something back?" look on their faces.

Or when they get back from school and you ask if they've had a good day and they grunt at you. So refreshing. But you are still incredibly pleased to see them—for them, you are their someone or something.

And no, the red light of the TV standby button isn't enough. You do need a person or a pet. One of my sons claims his gecko is always pleased to see him, but I have tried hard to detect any emotion on its face and so far failed—the gecko's, not my son's.

---

* Not taking them on a long enough walk because you've been so busy, forgetting biscuits, stuff like that. I don't mean treating them really badly. Who would do that?

132    THE RULES OF LIFE

Having someone or something who is pleased to see you is important because it gives you someone who needs you, and this gives you a purpose, stops you getting self-absorbed, gives you a reason for getting on with life. But what if you live alone and don't have pets or children? Well, volunteer or charity work is a very good way to quickly get in the situation where somebody is pleased to see you. Then again, it could be right on your doorstep.

Even living alone in a part of London where people never really talked to their neighbors, a friend of mine discovered there was a disabled retired man who lived a few doors down from her. She noticed that he found excuses to "just happen to be at his door" as she walked past on her way back from work most days. He was clearly a bit lonely and really valued a quick chat (or a longer one if possible). He was pleased to see her. Who is pleased to see you?

WE ALL NEED
SOMEONE WHO IS
PLEASED TO SEE US.
IT MAKES US FEEL IT IS
ALL WORTHWHILE.

# RULE 64

## Know When to Listen and When to Act

I don't know if it's harder for us men to learn this one, but I find it tough. Whenever anyone has a problem, I want to rush off and do something. Doesn't really matter what, just so long as I am doing something, anything.

In actual fact, what is often required of me is that I sit down and listen. I am not being told my wife's troubles and problems just so I can be all macho and rescue her or leap to her defense or single-handedly take on the world for her (in fact, be a hero). What is needed is a sympathetic ear, a shoulder perhaps to cry on, an "Oh, that must be awful for you" sort of response, a counselor's approach, and a full and rapt attention with eye contact. That's the tricky bit. As soon as I've heard the problem, I've switched off, or rather I've switched to working out what the solution must be.

But for me, when I have a problem I don't want to hear sympathetic noises and encouraging sounds. I don't want a heart space where I can share. I just want a solution, an offer of help, an extra pair of hands, a stout length of rope, and a screwdriver.*

But then all my problems are object related and need practical solutions—a guy's sort of thing. All the problems that I find the hardest to just listen to are person related and need a completely different approach. Knowing when to listen and when to act is an extremely useful skill to develop. I still constantly need to sit on my hands though to stop someone sharing

---

* Or whatever it takes to fix my particular problem.

a problem with me by saying, "Hold it right there; I can see exactly what this needs" and then rushing off to fetch my tool kit.

Of course, some problems don't actually have solutions; that's not why we're being told them. We are being told so we can be part of the process, and that may be sympathy, grief, shock, empathy, kindness, emotional advice, or hand-holding. Knowing when to offer chocolate and sympathy or a tool kit and a stout rope instead is the skill to learn, and a good Rules Player gets it right. (Yes, yes, I know; I still get it wrong far too often.)

KNOWING WHEN TO OFFER
CHOCOLATE AND
SYMPATHY OR A TOOL KIT
AND A STOUT ROPE
INSTEAD IS THE SKILL
TO LEARN.

# RULE 65

## Have a Passion for Your Life Together

So you two met and fell in love and resolved to spend your lives together. And you are, I hope. But at what level? I'm not being funny here, but serious (for once). Just sort of living together, going through the days, not really connecting isn't good enough, I'm afraid. You have to have a passion for your life together. A what? A passion. Being together has to be a strong bond, a common sharing of experience, a dream-fulfilling romance that carries you both along. Love isn't for the half dead, the sound asleep (or even the merely dozing off), the can't-be-bothered-to-make-the-effort-anymore. You have to make the effort. You have to stay awake, in touch, in tune. You have to share dreams and goals and ambitions and plans. You have to have passion for being with each other.

Look, I know that all relationships go through peaks and troughs. I know we get complacent and even a little bored at times. But you are dedicating your life to someone else's happiness in a way, and that requires focus, strength, passion, drive, enthusiasm, and effort. What's that? You're not dedicating yourself to someone else's happiness? Then what are you doing? That's what a relationship is all about in a sense. And if you're not doing that, what do you think you are doing?

You have to really care, to still be in love, to want your partner to be fulfilled, successful, happy, complete.

In an ideal world, you only get one crack of the whip at this. (I know that lots of people have several partners over a lifetime, but I assume the aim is always to stay together for life and not to get divorced.) This is your chance to have a really good, strong relationship based on mutual trust, responsibility, shared happiness, drive, and the pursuit of excellence. It isn't? What is it then? It has to be if you are going to get the maximum out of it. Your partner isn't just there for someone to chat with when you get a bit fed up and want some company. She is there because she loves you and you her. She is there for you both to have a relationship. If that isn't as much as anyone needs as an incentive to live life to the full and have a passion, then I don't know what is.

...YOU ARE DEDICATING
YOUR LIFE TO SOMEONE
ELSE'S HAPPINESS.

# RULE 66

## Make Sure Your Love Making is Making Love

So! We get to talk about sex now? Well, actually no. What I'm going to talk about is love. If you are in love and being loved, it is part of the natural process to make love, and this is both fun and fraught with all sorts of problems. In a relationship, as successful Rules Players, we have to be kind, courteous, reverential, stimulating, creative, respectful, thoughtful, considerate, and sexual. Within that sexual relationship we have to be all those things as well—respectful, kind, etc. We have to take our partner's needs and wants into consideration without subjecting ourselves to anything we wouldn't want to do or find embarrassing or difficult. We have the right to privacy. We have the right to respect. We have the right to be held in high esteem.

And so does our partner. Consideration has to be the key word. We have to be considerate of what our partner needs, likes, wants, is capable of doing. We have to be courteous.

And yes, within all this there is a space and a place for passion, for excitement, for rude raunchy sex. We don't have to be tame to be considerate, we don't have to be inhibited to be kind, we don't have to be tame just because we are being respectful. This isn't about being unexciting or dreary or boring just because we are taking our partner's safety, privacy, health, intimacy into account. Even the most passionate lovers can be kind to each other while tearing each other's clothes off and having very physical sex—the two can go together.

Having sex with someone you love—making love if you like— is an honor in a way. (For me, just having someone these days who is prepared to take her clothes off at the same time as I do is an honor….) Making love is as close as we are ever going to get to another human being, as intimate as it is ever going to be. If we don't move respectfully in this arena, then what are we doing? And respect grows out of knowledge—knowledge of not only what our partner likes best but of the whole process. We should be as skilful as possible, and if we aren't, it is something we can spend a bit of time learning about. There is no shame in learning. We can't all be born the best drivers and the best lovers in the world.

WE HAVE THE RIGHT
TO PRIVACY, TO RESPECT,
TO BE HELD IN
HIGH ESTEEM.

# RULE 67

## Keep Talking

Yep, you've gotta keep talking. When there is trouble afoot, it's talking that will get us out of it. When we are going through bad patches, it is talking it out that will see us through. When we are optimistic and excited, it is talking that will help our partner share it.

If we aren't talking, there is something wrong. If we aren't talking, what are we doing? Talking helps us understand, listen, share, communicate.

Lots of people assume that silence means there's a problem, something wrong. Of course, we don't need to fill all the silences, but there are some pretty basic rules of etiquette when it comes to talking to each other:

- Acknowledge that your partner has spoken to you—and no, a grunt or a sigh isn't what I mean.

- Make some recognition every few seconds that you are still awake, alive, in the room, interested, paying attention—this may be a nod, a yes or no, a noise of encouragement (hmm, oh).

- Be aware that talking is part of your duties as a lover/partner, and you should be good at it.

- Good talking leads to good sex—if you aren't talking, you aren't flirting, holding hands, seducing. By talking, we are committing the act known as foreplay.

- Talking helps resolve problems; silence only amplifies them.

- Talking keeps you together—it's what you used to do when you first fell in love, remember?

There is obviously a time and a place for silences (see Rule 58)—but talking is healthy, productive, companionable, friendly, loving, kind, and fun. Silences can be boring, unhelpful, destructive, and threatening. Obviously, there is quality talking and there is rambling on. Make sure you don't just chatter away to fill the silences with meaningless trivia. Talking has to have some purpose, although gossiping is fine. Just babbling isn't. So talk sensibly now.

> IF WE AREN'T TALKING,
> THERE IS SOMETHING
> WRONG.
> IF WE AREN'T TALKING,
> WHAT ARE WE DOING?

# RULE 68

## Respect Privacy

"I want to be alone...." Each and every one of us has a God-given right to respect, privacy, trust, honesty. But of all of them, it is privacy that is the most sacrosanct, inviolate, untouchable.

You must respect your partner's privacy, as she must yours. If you don't, you have to question all those other things—trust, respect, honesty—as well. If they are all missing, what you've got there isn't a relationship and, quite frankly, I don't know what it is, except it belongs in the morgue. So we'll assume you have a good and healthy relationship. This means you have respect for your partner's privacy. In all areas.

If your partner chooses not to discuss something with you, then that is her right, and you do not have the right to:

- Wheedle
- Threaten
- Emotionally blackmail
- Bribe
- Withhold privileges
- Try and find out by underhand means and methods

And no, charming your partner out of it counts as a no-no as well. Privacy isn't just about not opening someone's mail or listening to her telephone messages or reading her emails when she's not looking. Privacy is also about making sure your partner can carry out her ablutions on her own—we all need a certain degree of grace and dignity in our lives, and separate bathroom activities is the standard bottom line actually.

Sharing a bathroom all the time isn't desirable, at least not for all activities. Ugh, how horrid. If you can't have separate bathrooms, at least have some separate privacy in the bathroom. I know, shared baths and the like can be very intimate and romantic, but you don't have to cut your toenails or squeeze your blackheads in front of each other. Don't do it. Winston Churchill said the reason he managed to stay married for 56 years—or however long it was—was separate bathrooms. So keep yourself to yourself in your more intimate ablutions, and make sure you don't intrude on anyone else's privacy. You can extend this Rule to everyone else in the entire universe, not just your partner.

If you feel a need to intrude on someone else's privacy, you have to take a long hard look at yourself and fathom out why. The truth may be unpalatable, but you have to know it.

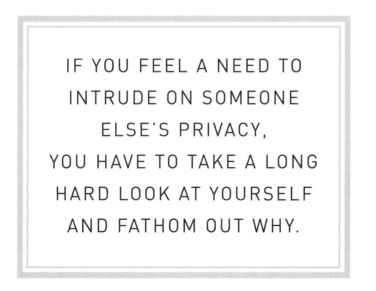

IF YOU FEEL A NEED TO
INTRUDE ON SOMEONE
ELSE'S PRIVACY,
YOU HAVE TO TAKE A LONG
HARD LOOK AT YOURSELF
AND FATHOM OUT WHY.

# RULE 69

## Check You Both Have the Same Shared Goals

When we first meet and fall in love, we think we know pretty well everything we can about our love. We have so much in common. It all seems so easy, so intuitive, so natural. Of course we want the same. Of course we are two sides of the same coin. Of course we are going to share life's highway together.

Wrong, wrong, wrong. The highway will diverge at times, and if you aren't on the ball, you will lose sight of each other completely and forever. You have to keep checking that you are both using the same map so to speak, both heading for the same destination, both going in the same direction even.

So what are your shared goals? Where do you both think you're going? No, don't guess here. Don't make them assumed goals or even guessed goals. You have to know what your partner thinks are the shared goals—and what you think. They might be a world apart. Or then again they might be very close. You'll only know if you ask, discreetly of course. Don't want to frighten the horses here.

And you have to differentiate between shared goals and shared dreams. We all have dreams—the cottage by the sea, the trip round the world, the Ferrari, the second home in Malibu, the purpose-built wine cellar (fully stocked, of course), the Olympic-size swimming pool—but goals are different. Goals are to have children (or not); to travel a lot; to retire early and live in Spain; to bring up the children to be happy, well-adjusted people; to stay together (!); to move to the countryside/town; to downsize together and work from home; to run your own business together; to get a dog. I guess dreams are things you aim to get one day, and goals are what you are doing together. Dreams are acquisitions that either of you could want, and goals are shared aims that you need each other for, because without the other the goal is pretty meaningless.

This Rule is about reviewing. To review, you have to talk to your partner about where it is you both think you're going and what you're doing. It doesn't have to be heavy. This can be a light review just to touch base and check that you are both on the same track. It doesn't have to be too detailed, just simple questions to confirm a general similar direction, rather than trying to map out an A-to-Z of your future life together.

YOU HAVE TO KEEP
CHECKING
THAT YOU ARE BOTH
USING THE SAME MAP.

# RULE 70

## Treat Your Partner Better Than Your Best Friend

I was talking to a friend about this Rule the other day, and she disagreed with me emphatically. She said you had to treat your friends better because you knew them better and you owed them more loyalty. I then went on to talk to another friend, and she said that wasn't the case. You treated your partner better because you knew them less well. Intriguing. My point is you should treat your partner better than your friends because your partner is both lover and friend. And ideally best friend.

If your partner is not your best friend, then who is? And why? Is it because your partner is the opposite sex and you need a same-sex best friend? Or your partner is the same sex and you need an opposite-sex best friend? Is it because you don't see a lover as a friend? (If you do answer yes to this, what do you see your partner as...what is his role or function in being your partner?)

Again, all this is about being conscious. Treating your partner better than your best friend means you have given it some thought and made a conscious decision to do so—or not if it's the case.

I would have thought treating your partner better than your best friend would have been a given. This means not interfering, respecting his privacy, treating him like an independent grown-up. You only have to look around to see couples who treat each other like small children, nagging, scolding, arguing, criticizing, nit-picking. They wouldn't do it with their friends, so why do they do it with the one person who is supposed to mean heaven and earth to them?

I'll give you an example. You are a passenger in a car being driven by a friend. She makes a foolish error (though not a dangerous one). You would probably start teasing and laugh a lot. Now imagine the same scenario but with your partner who has messed up. Do you:

- Make him feel very small?
- Not let him forget it in a long while?
- Tell everyone else?
- Take over the driving for a while on the grounds he's not to be trusted?
- Treat him the same as you would a friend and laugh a lot?

Hopefully the last one, but watch other couples in similar situations and see what they do.

WHAT YOU DO SEE YOUR
PARTNER AS...WHAT IS
HIS ROLE OR FUNCTION
IN BEING
YOUR PARTNER?

# RULE 71

## Contentment Is a High Aim

If you ask a lot of people what they want in life, they say, "Oh, just to be happy, I guess." Same goes if you ask what they want for their children, "I don't mind what they do as long as they are happy." You'd be better off wishing that you or your children could be astronauts or brain surgeons—at least you're in with a sporting chance then. You can train. They can qualify.

Happiness is such an illusory thing that spending too much time chasing it is not very worthwhile. Happiness is one end of a spectrum—misery being the other end. It is a state of extreme, just as misery represents the other end. If you check back at the times in your life when you've been happy—or thought you might have been—I'll bet there were other extreme feelings involved. The birth of a child? Excitement yes. Wonder yes. Relief at a successful birth. Yes. But happiness? I'm not sure.

People think they'll be happy on vacation when they mean relaxed or stimulated or freed from their cares—and indeed they are. Aiming for happiness is one of those "bigger is best" things. You're never going to make it because there is no top end limit. You just have to go on aiming for even bigger all the time. Instead of aiming for happy, it's better to aim for contentment. Now that's attainable. That's a worthy goal.

This applies especially to relationships—both to the quest to find Mr. or Mrs. Right and in what happens when you do. Most of us want to fall madly head-over-heels in love. Big chemistry—fireworks, butterflies, unbelievable feelings. It's brilliant. It's extreme. But that intensity can't and won't last. You have to go back to reality sometime. You have to get on with your life. No one can live at that intensity, that lofty altitude all the time. Contentment is what you hope for after the elation has worn off and you settle back into a relaxed and happy simplicity. In fact, contentment is the worthier aim, because it lasts.

And so if you find you are with somebody where there is no big firework display, palpitations, and extreme of feelings but there is a baseline contentment and warmth and love—be happy with that.

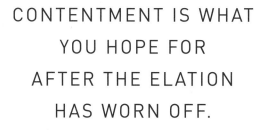

CONTENTMENT IS WHAT
YOU HOPE FOR
AFTER THE ELATION
HAS WORN OFF.

# RULE 72

## You Don't Both Have to Have the Same Rules

Lots of couples make the assumption that everything has to be the same for both of them—that you have to have the same set of rules for both partners. Not true. You can operate under different rules for important areas. The happiest relationships, the most successful, the strongest, are where both parties see the need for flexibility in their rules and adjust their relationship accordingly.

I expect you want an example? Of course you do. Let's suppose one of you is fanatically tidy and the other fanatically messy (whatever that is). Normally, you would have one complaining to the other all the time about how messy/tidy the other is. There would be arguments and problems. That's because you are both trying to work to the same rule—we both have to be tidy/we both have to be messy. How about a different rule? I can be messy; you can be tidy. I can have areas where I can be messy, and you have areas where you can be tidy. Now we don't argue because we have a different rule. I don't have to be tidy when it isn't in my nature, and you don't have to be messy when it isn't in your nature.

Another example? My wife hates being teased, and she hates being tickled. Me? I'm not bothered. She has the rule that she is not to be tickled—or teased—and my rule is I can.* You may be the kind of person who wants to know where your partner is, whereas your partner is not bothered about where you are and doesn't expect you to report on it. You can then have a rule where your partner tells you where she's going, to

---

* No, this is only for my wife. Of course, you can't come round and tickle or tease me.

reassure you, but you don't need to keep her completely in the picture because she doesn't worry about it.

Your partner may need constant reassurance that you love them and may need to be told several times a day. You might prefer to be told less frequently but when it's genuinely felt—so you would have a rule that you'd mention it often, but she didn't have to say it back every time. Different strokes for different folks.

THE HAPPIEST
RELATIONSHIPS ARE
WHERE BOTH PARTIES
SEE THE NEED FOR
FLEXIBILITY IN
THEIR RULES.

# PART III

---

# FAMILY AND FRIENDS RULES

If you imagine yourself as the center of your own universe, then you are the very hub. The next circle around you is your lover, your partner; this is your closest, most intimate relationship. The next circle to that is your family and friends. These are the people you love the most, choose to spend the most time with, love you the most. These are the people you can relax with, kick off your shoes and be yourself. But there are still Rules. There is still a right way to treat them and a not-so-right way. You still have to behave with honor, dignity, respect. You have responsibilities toward both your children and your parents. You have a duty to your siblings. You have obligations, that have to be taken seriously, to your friends.

You have a whole raft of hats to wear—parent, friend, child, brother/sister, uncle/aunt, godparent, niece/nephew, cousin—and a whole set of rules and duties to perform. The next section is guidance on how best to wear all these hats.

As we go through this life, we have to interact with other people. We rub up against them (emotionally) all the time, and we have to have rules to govern our behavior so we do right by them, to steer us through tricky situations, new experiences, and ongoing close relationships.

If we want our relationships with our family and friends to be successful and for them to think the very best of us, then we do need to give those relationships some thought—a conscious approach rather than sailing on asleep at the wheel like most people. By consciously being aware of what we are doing, we can improve those relationships, iron out the problems, encourage others, and generally spread a bit of warmth and happiness as we go. What could be finer?

# RULE 73

## If You Are Going to Be a Friend, Be a Good Friend

Being a real friend is a tremendous responsibility. You have to be loyal, honest (but not too honest), sincere, reliable, dependable, friendly (stands to reason really), pleasant, open, sociable (not much point having friends if you're not going to be sociable, is there?), responsive, welcoming, and gracious. You also have to be forgiving at times, be prepared to offer help, support, and sympathy. At the same time, you don't want to be taken advantage of or have the wool pulled over your eyes. And you may have to be brutally candid at times and be prepared to risk the friendship by being so. Yet equally there are times you need to hold your tongue and keep your opinion to yourself. They are your friends, not clones of you—they do things differently. You have to be counselor, confessor, priest, helper, companion, friend, confidant(e), and comrade. You have to offer the friendship enthusiasm, dedication, determination, creativity, interest, passion, and drive.

And this is all what you have to do. What does your friend have to do? Well, in an ideal world the same. If your friend fails to do any of this, you will still carry on being her friend, being forgiving, being supportive, and being there.

And I guess if you have to take anything away from this Rule, the most important bit is being there. You are there when your friend is going through it and not just there for the good times. You will be there when your friend needs you in the early hours, the dark days, the times of trouble and stress. You will be there to hold her hand, let her cry on your shoulder, lend her a Kleenex, pat her on the back and make her endless cups of coffee. And you will tell them to cheer up, stop worrying, stop being such a fool, whatever it takes to get them up and at it again.

You will be there to give your friend good advice. You will be there just to listen at times. You will be there when you don't want to be. You will be there when all her other friends have fallen by the wayside. You will be there no matter what.

Someone once said that a real friend is someone you can be having a conversation with as she gets on a plane, you don't see her for ten years, and when she arrives back you carry on the conversation as she gets off the plane like a moment hadn't passed. That's exactly how it is between good friends.

THE MOST IMPORTANT BIT IS BEING THERE...AND NOT JUST FOR THE GOOD TIMES.

# RULE 74

## Never Be Too Busy for Loved Ones

It is very easy in the rush of living to overlook people close to us. I do it. I have brothers who are very special, very close to me, and I forget to phone, forget to stay in touch. Not because I don't care but because I am too busy. Unforgivable. Every now and then I'll complain that I haven't heard from them. But, of course, it is me not staying in touch just as much as it is them. We have to make time, because if we don't, time slips past so fast that a few weeks become months, and then years are added on before we know it.

It's the same with children. Parents all harbor a secret fantasy of, "Wouldn't it be nice to return to the Victorian ideal of seeing them for an hour before bedtime when the nanny has them all bathed and pajama-ed and ready with the cookies and milk?" sort of thing. Well, I know I do even if you don't. But the more time we put into our relationships—with children, siblings, parents, friends—the more we get out of them. It has to be us to make the move, to phone, to stay in touch. And what if they don't also do this? Fine. You're now the Rules Player.

This is what you do. You become incredibly successful at handling your life, at processing guilt (you don't have any because you phoned, you wrote, you stayed in touch), at forgiveness (they didn't phone or write or stay in touch), at relationships in general. You take the moral high ground and be the first to offer the hand of friendship, be the first to forgive and forget. (And I don't care how serious the squabble was, Rules Players don't carry grudges, ever....)

No matter how busy your life is—and hopefully these Rules will eliminate some stress and free up some time—you have to make time. You have to make quality time (sorry, I hate that expression as well) for all those around you to whom you make a difference. Those who love you get repaid in time—it's a fair exchange. They love you, and you give them something of yourself, something precious. Yep, your time and attention. And you do this willingly, not as a chore. You do this with dedication and commitment and wholehearted enthusiasm—or you don't do it at all. There is no point spending quality time with your kids, for example, and using that time to catch up on work or read the paper or get tomorrow's lunchboxes ready. You have to be there entirely for them, or they'll know your attention is elsewhere and they'll feel cheated.

So when the phone rings and it's your mom, your grandmother, or your old friend but you're really busy doing something, don't keep her on the phone making "uh huh" noises while you simultaneously finish searching the web or writing that letter. Either put everything down and give her your full attention, or ask if you can call her back later—and make sure you do. One day she might not be there—and then you will so desperately wish you'd actually listened. But then it'll be too late. So make time for the people who matter—today.

> THE MORE WE PUT INTO
> OUR RELATIONSHIPS,
> THE MORE WE
> GET OUT OF THEM.

# RULE 75

## Let Your Kids Mess Up for Themselves—They Don't Need Any Help from You

I have children, and I naturally want them to be happy and well adjusted and successful. But do I also harbor secret plans for them? Do I want them to be doctors? Lawyers? Diplomats? Scientists? Archaeologists? Paleontologists? Writers? Entrepreneurs? The Pope? (Look, someone has to be the Pope, and it may be some parent's ambition somewhere to see his child as the Pope.) Astronauts?

No. I don't think so. Hand on my heart, I can say I haven't ever had such ambitions for them. I do hope they're not listening, but I can say that I've been disappointed on the odd occasion when their career choice has seemed a bit unusual—not their sort of thing at all. But you have to let them make mistakes. You can't steer them right all the time, or they'd never learn for themselves.

And this is what this Rule is all about—giving your kids the space to mess things up. We've all done it. I was given immense freedom to screw up, and I did it big time, magnificently, spectacularly. Result? I learned pretty quickly what worked and what didn't. I have a cousin who wasn't given anything like the same freedom. He was much more protected, and he didn't screw up anywhere nearly so badly. But later in life, and he'd be the first to agree with this, he managed his life in such an unfortunate way that his screw-up really was spectacular. We all have to make mistakes. Better to make them while we're young and have the resiliency to bounce back.

Being a parent is about 75 percent making it up as you go along. You too have the freedom to make mistakes. Trouble is that if you get it wrong as a parent, your mistakes can really affect someone's life adversely. That's why it can be really hard to stand back and watch our children make bad choices. We want to run to them and protect them, nurture them a bit more, and keep them from harm. But they have to learn by getting it wrong. If we think they'll only learn by us telling them, then we are making a big mistake. They have to do life for themselves to really get to grips with it. It's real, and they can't learn it from a book or from us or from the television. They can only learn it by getting their fingers burned. Your job is to stand by with the bandaids and the antiseptic and a kiss to make it better.

You are, of course, allowed to ask leading questions: Are you sure that's a good idea? Have you thought this one through? And what happens after you've done that? Can you afford to take that much time off? Won't it hurt a bit? Didn't you try something like this before? You can also do this with friends as well when you can see they are about to make a big mistake but you don't want to be the killjoy. Try not to make your questions sound too judgmental or moany, or they'll ignore you and go ahead just to be stubborn.

> YOU CAN'T STEER THEM
> RIGHT ALL THE TIME, OR
> THEY'D NEVER LEARN FOR
> THEMSELVES.

# RULE 76

## Have a Little Respect and Forgiveness for Your Parents

This one may or may not affect you. Personally, as I am now technically an orphan, it shouldn't affect me. But it does. Big time. I was brought up with two major dysfunctional attributes. A missing father and a difficult mother. I have siblings with the same background. We have all handled it differently. I found it easier to come to terms with my mother once I too had children and could see what a difficult job it is. I could then also see that some people are intuitively, naturally good at it. And some people are, to be brutally frank, utterly useless at it. My mother fell into the latter category. Was that her fault? No. Should I blame her? No. Can I forgive her? There is nothing to forgive. She embarked on a life path for which she was ill equipped, received no help, was lacking in any skill, and found extremely limiting and difficult. Result? She treated her children appallingly, and we probably all need therapy. Or forgiveness and respect. Why should she be blamed for doing a difficult job badly? Hey, there are lots of areas in all our lives where we aren't very efficient or skilled or even enthusiastic.

Your parents do the best they can. And that might not be good enough for you, but it is still the best they could do. They can't be blamed if they weren't very good at it. We can't all be fabulous parents.

And the absent father? That's OK, too. We all make choices that others can judge as bad or unforgivable or just plain selfish and wrong. But we aren't there. We don't know what weaknesses people have or what drives them. Or indeed what is even going through their head. We can't judge until we, too, have to make the same choice. And even then if we choose a different way, then that's fine, but we still can't judge or blame.

So, for the fact your parents brought you into the world, have a little respect and forgiveness. If they did a good job, then tell them. If you love them (and there is nothing that says you have to), then tell them. And if they were appalling at parenting, then forgive them and move on.

As offspring, you do have a duty to be respectful. You have a responsibility to treat your parents kindly and be more than they are by being forgiving and nonjudgmental. You can rise above your upbringing.

HEY, THERE ARE LOTS OF
AREAS IN ALL OUR LIVES
WHERE WE AREN'T VERY
EFFICIENT OR SKILLED OR
EVEN ENTHUSIASTIC.

## Give Your Kids a Break

We'll talk in a bit about what good parenting is—what your role as a parent is. First, let's look at this Rule—give your kids a break means support and encourage your children. In fact this should be support and encourage all children, not just your own. Children get a pretty poor deal of it. They hear it from all directions, and the word that figures most in their lives is "no." No, you can't do this. No, you're not old enough for this. No, you can't have that. No, you're not going there. No, you can't see that film.

Cast your mind back, and see if it wasn't the same for you.

"No" is terribly easy for us to say. It's the word that trips so readily off the tongue. But to give support and encouragement, we do have to train ourselves out of it. We have to learn to say "yes." Obviously we need to qualify our "yes," depending on the age or skills or development of the child. But a resounding "yes" gives kids a great boost even if it is followed by a "but not at the moment," or "when you are old enough" or "when you have saved up."

It is also easy to say to a child, "You're not very good at that," or "I wouldn't do that if I were you; you'll only fail." Better to encourage a child and let him learn that he might fail than to set the idea running in his mind beforehand. I know we all want to protect kids from harm, from failure, from disappoint-ment. But sometimes we have to push them forward and shelve those worries for the moment.

Truly successful parents are the ones saying, "Go on, you can do that, you'll be great at that, you'll be terrific." By voicing such positive enforcement, our children get to believe in themselves and can do more, be more, achieve more. If we just say "no," they'll grow up with low self-esteem and lacking in confidence.

A friend recalls how she desperately wanted to be a ballet dancer when she was 6 years old. She was already showing the signs of being destined for her current 6 ft tall, large feet, athletic build—as far from a ballet dancer as you can imagine. Her parents must have been able to see this and could have told her that really she should do something else. Like all-in wrestling for kids. But instead, they found her a ballet class. It didn't take long for her to realize that ballet wasn't right for her, and she stopped going because it made her legs hurt. However, it was her choice to stop. And she left with her self-esteem intact. (She only wishes they hadn't taken the photos.)

Whatever kids want to do, it is not your job to edit their dream, stand in their way, voice your concerns, limit their hopes or discourage them in any way. Your job is to give guidance while supporting and encouraging. Your job is to give them the resources to achieve whatever it is they want to. Whether they do or don't achieve is irrelevant. If they had the chance, that's everything.

> THEY HEAR IT FROM ALL DIRECTIONS, AND THE WORD THAT FIGURES MOST IN THEIR LIVES IS "NO."

## Never Lend Money Unless You Are Prepared to Write It Off

The full title of this Rule should actually be: Never lend money—to your friend or children, or your siblings, or even parents—unless you are prepared to write off either the money or the relationship.

There is a lovely story told, I think, about Oscar Wilde (correct me if I've got the wrong person) who borrowed a book from a friend and forgot to return it. His friend turned up and demanded the book back, by which time young Oscar had lost it. His friend asked Oscar if he wasn't jeopardizing the friendship by not returning the book. Oscar Wilde merely replied, "Yes. But aren't you also doing the same thing by demanding it back?"

If you lend money—or a book or anything else—don't do it unless you are prepared for it to be lost, forgotten, not returned, broken, ignored, whatever.

If you are precious about it, then don't lend it in the first place. If it means a lot to you, keep it safe. If you do lend anything, including money, then don't expect to get it back if you value the friendship—or relationship. If you do get it back, then that is a bonus. If you don't, well you were prepared for that in the first place.

Lots of parents make the mistake of lending money to their children and then getting all hurt and disappointed when they don't get repaid. But they have spent the child's entire life giving them money, and then as soon as they get a bit grown up and go away to college or whatever, the parents suddenly start saying it's a loan and demanding repayment. Of course the child isn't going to repay it. She hasn't been trained to. It is unrealistic to expect her to do so. If she does do, count your blessings and be grateful for the bonus.

Same with friends. Don't lend them anything if the nonreturn is going to matter to you. It is your choice, after all. You don't have to lend anything to anyone. If you choose to do so, be prepared to write it off or don't do it. Obviously, if the money means more to you than the friendship, then of course demand it to be repaid—and add interest as well.

And the same goes for siblings or parents. (Goodness, don't ever lend money to them; they'll never pay it back.) So who should you lend money to? Strangers, of course. And they won't pay it back either.

IF YOU ARE PRECIOUS
ABOUT IT,
THEN DON'T LEND IT
IN THE FIRST PLACE.

# RULE 79

## Keep Quiet

I have a friend who has three small children. She told me recently that before she had children, she didn't really get the things that people with children told her. She wasn't always convinced by their claims of tiredness or logistical problems, she didn't necessarily believe that children could squabble that much or be such hard work, she sometimes just didn't understand what they were talking about. Even when she had two children, she didn't really get what people with more than two children were telling her. Now, however, she says she finally really gets it, and it just isn't like she'd imagined.

You'd have thought that if you had two children you'd know what life was like for people with three kids. But you don't. In fact, you don't even know what life is like for other people with two children who are different sexes from yours, or further apart in age, or when there's less money, or the parents are working different hours from you. Even apparently similar circumstances can be deceptively different.

And we all have our own personalities and values and strengths and weaknesses. I know one person who is widowed and hates spending time with happy couples because it reminds her what she's lost. I have another widowed friend who has no problem spending time with couples because she doesn't see it in relation to her own marriage. Neither is right or wrong, but both have their own histories and attitudes.

So what am I saying? Essentially, don't judge. Try walking a mile in someone else's moccasins before you presume to know what his life is like. My own mother had one of her children adopted when he was a few weeks old. For years I thought this was a terrible thing to do. But once I had children of my own, I realized that I had no way of assessing whether what she did was OK. She already had five children, she was widowed, and therefore the sole earner (in the 1950s, when that was even harder than it is now), and she was working all hours with no money for childcare. Would I have coped any better in her circumstances? I can't know.

This isn't easy. I'm not just saying that we should think twice before we form an opinion. I'm also saying that since we can't judge anyone else's situation, we should keep quiet about their choices in life. It's not for us to tell even our nearest and dearest how we think they should act. For many of us, and I'm certainly including myself here, this can be one of the hardest Rules of all.

However, think about how you feel when people try to tell you what to do. If you know what's right for you, you don't appreciate other people telling you what they think. They don't understand. No, not even your closest family members really understand what it's like to be you. Even if you're making a mistake, you still want to be allowed to make it for yourself and to learn from it. And that's how we need to treat everyone else around us. Tough, ain't it? But necessary.

> THINK ABOUT HOW YOU
> FEEL WHEN PEOPLE TRY
> TO TELL YOU WHAT TO DO.

# RULE 80

# There Are No Bad Children

There are no bad children. Yes, there may be children who do bad things. There may be children who do appalling things. But they are not bad. No matter how naughty my children are, they are not bad. They may make me climb the walls with their behavior at times, but when they have gone to sleep and I peep in at them, they are angelic little cherubs, utterly good, utterly perfect. Yes, what they do during the day, to get my dander up, may be naughty, may be bad behavior, but they remain intrinsically good.

The only reason the behavior is bad is because they are exploring the world and learning where the boundaries are. They have to make mistakes in order to find out what's what. It is only natural and quite normal.

The same goes for any other behavior that is out of the ordinary. There are no clumsy children, only clumsy behavior. There are no stupid children, only stupid conduct. They are no spiteful children, only spiteful acts. There are no selfish children, only selfish actions.

Kids don't know any better, and it is your job to teach them, educate them, help them, encourage them. You start off on the wrong foot if you start off believing they are bad. You're almost bound to fail if you believe them to be faulty. You can't change a bad child, but you can change bad behavior. If you believe the child is good, you're on to a winner immediately. All you've got to do is change the behavior, and that is an attainable goal.

It is awfully detrimental to say to a child, "You are a bad child." It sets something up in their mind that is hard to shift. Better to say, "You've done a naughty thing," or "You've been naughty." This they can do something about. But if you tell them they are bad, there is nothing they can do about that, and it affects them.

YOU CAN'T CHANGE A
BAD CHILD,
BUT YOU CAN CHANGE
BAD BEHAVIOR.

# RULE 81

## Be Up Around People You Love

Your job from now on, as a Rules Player, is to be up around people you love. No more moaning. No more complaining. No more grumbling. These things will no more issue from your lips. You are, from now on, the positive one, the perpetually cheerful, always up one around whom good things revolve and happen.

When asked how are you, instead of saying, "Can't complain, mustn't grumble," in the future you will say, "Fine, good, marvelous"—No matter how crummy you feel, no matter what sort of a day you've had, no matter how low, down, or fed up you are. And do you know, the interesting thing is that when you do say "Marvelous," even if you don't feel it, you'll find something positive to say to follow it up with. Whereas if you'd said "Been better," then the follow-up thoughts would be negative. Try it—honestly, it really works.

In the future, right from today, from this very second, you have to become the one who is always happy, up, cheerful. Why? Because someone has to, or everybody will want to end it all. This life is hard and treacherous. Someone has to lift the burden, lift the spirits, lift the gloom. So who's it going to be? You, that's who.

I know, I know. You'll be sitting there reading this, thinking, "Why me? Why lay this burden on me?" Because you can do it, that's why. But do it secretly (remember Rule 1), without fuss or bother. Just a simple change of heart, change of direction. From now on you cannot be anything but up around those you love. OK, moan to strangers. But loved ones get the full treatment. Up, up, and away.

Successful people, those who have got it licked, are invariably cheerful. They care more about what people around them are going through, feeling, suffering than their own petty problems. They invariably want to know what's wrong with you rather than moaning about their day. They think positively, act positively, project confidence, verve, and enthusiasm.

I had a friend who went to live abroad in a country where he spoke very little of the language. But he said his mood lifted whenever he was there because he didn't know the words for fed up or miserable or down. When someone asked him how he was, he could only say "Happy," because that was the only word he knew to reply with. He found that when he said it, he felt it.

SOMEONE HAS TO
LIFT THE BURDEN,
LIFT THE SPIRITS,
LIFT THE GLOOM.

## Give Your Kids Responsibilities

Children grow up and leave home. They go from helpless babies to mature adults who have sex and drink beer while your back is turned. The secret is to try and keep pace with them. As they grow, you have to back off more and let them do more. You have to resist the urge to do everything for them and let them fry eggs* or paint dustbins** for themselves.

It's a delicate balancing act. You can't give kids more responsibility than they can handle, but at the same time you can't hold them back. And when you do let them fry eggs or paint dustbins for the first time, they are going to make a mess— yolk on the stove, paint on the garage floor. It's the mess most often that makes a parent say, "No, you can't." But we have to break a few eggs (ha ha) to be able to fry one. We have to gloop a bit of paint if kids are going to be able to carry out any DIY job for themselves when they are grown up.

When kids are tiny and learning to drink from a cup for the first time we expect spillage. We stand there with a paper towel in our hand prepared to mop up. But by the time they are teenagers, we've forgotten the art of hiding the paper towel

---

\* This one comes from my own son who, when he was asked what being a grown-up meant, said it was being able to fry eggs as he wasn't allowed to— he was about 8 at the time. I felt so mean I got him cooking breakfast every day for a month until he was sick of frying eggs.

\*\* This came from a friend who was always angry with his father. When I asked him about his relationship, he complained that as a kid he was never allowed to do anything to help. He finally lost it with his father when his father was painting a dustbin and the kid wanted to help and his father said, "No." But why? It wouldn't have hurt. Why the father was painting a dustbin in the first place remains a mystery.

behind our back waiting for them to spill stuff. We expect them to be able to keep their room tidy the first time. But they've never done it before. They don't know how to do it. They have to learn, and part of that learning process is not doing it, doing it badly, doing it differently from how we, as adults would do it. Our job is to help them. To hand them responsibility slowly, bit by bit, but with guidance.

We expect kids to do everything right the first time, no spillage, no broken eggs, no paint on the floor. It is our expectations that are unrealistic. Growing up is a messy business.

AS THEY GROW,
YOU HAVE TO
BACK OFF MORE AND
LET THEM DO MORE.

## Your Children Need to Fall Out with You to Leave Home

Your kids have never tidied their room. They've played their music long and loud and driven you mad. You and your kids are about at a breaking point, and you wonder where you went wrong as a parent of sullen, moody, dressed-in-black teenagers. Your kids are monosyllabic, depressed (but miraculously cheer up when their friends come round), always hungry, rude, mercenary, troublesome, and unrelentlessly embarrassed by you. And you blame yourself. It is all your fault. You have somehow failed them. Rubbish. This is all good stuff.

Look, your kids have got to fall out with you to be able to leave home. If they loved you too much, they couldn't leave. You've nurtured them, wiped their bottom, dressed them, fed them, doled out money for all of their life. And they don't want to feel grateful. They want to leave, drink too much, have sex, and use grown-up swear words. They don't want to be your darling little angel anymore. They want to be irritating and daring and rude and adult. They want to discover and explore and get into trouble all by themselves. They need to break the chains, rip the parental ropes off, and run over the hill shouting that they are free at last. How on earth can they do that if they are still in awe of you, still feeling so attached to you, still loving you so much? They have to break free by not getting on with you before they can come home again as something more than just your child.

This process is all natural, and you should welcome it and be glad to see the back of them. Throw 'em out early, I say, and then they'll be back all the sooner. You can't ruffle their hair ever again or tuck them in or read them a story, but you will find a grown-up friend comes back, and you can share a whole new relationship with them.

Hold them back, and they'll resent you for longer. Take it personally, and they'll take longer to return because they'll feel guilty.

And you can show this to your teenager: Don't give your parents too hard a time. They are feeling just as threatened by this new relationship as you are. Give them a break. They're making it up as they go along, just as much as you are.

THEY HAVE TO
BREAK FREE BEFORE
THEY CAN COME HOME
AGAIN AS SOMETHING
MORE THAN JUST
YOUR CHILD.

# RULE 84

## Your Kids Will Have Friends You Don't Like

"Oh no, not Mickey Brown—again!" This was my mother's cry every Saturday morning. She hated Mickey Brown. Loathed and detested him with a vengeance. Why? I have no idea. She disliked most of my friends, but she saved up all the venom for poor Mickey Brown, whom she took against before she ever met him.

Look, your children will sometimes have friends you don't approve of. It's natural. Live with it. As kids, we are attracted to other kids who are different from us. It's our way of finding out. We go for the very poor kid or the very rich kid because we have no experience of it and want to know what it is like. We go for the ruffian or the spoiled princess or the kid from a different ethnic background to ours or the ragged urchin who smells or the autistic kid or the one from the gypsy encampment or the smug middle-class one whose parents are accountants.

Whatever it is, as parents, we will be tempted to disapprove. It's human nature, but we mustn't. We must be supportive, encouraging, welcoming, and open. Why? Because if our child is hanging out with other kids that test our tolerance, it's a good thing. It shows we are bringing them up not to be prejudiced or judgmental. And if they aren't acting this way, we shouldn't either.

The funny thing is that Mickey Brown's parents couldn't stand me either. He wasn't allowed to play with guns, and I was always smuggling them into his house when his parents weren't looking. I didn't like guns particularly—and we are talking cap guns here—but I did love getting him into trouble…

One of my own children had a birthday party and insisted on inviting a kid in his class who had serious adjustment problems (what we used to call a "naughty child" but you can't do that any more—see Rule 73). When his parents came to collect him, they were quite tearful, as it was the first birthday party this poor kid had ever been invited to. What's that? His behavior? Oh, he was a little angel and didn't put a foot wrong. In your dreams. He behaved true to type, and I was heard muttering, "Never again; he never comes here again," for many weeks afterward. No, seriously he played up a bit and wrecked the place, but no more than any of the others did. One of the others, a supposedly good kid, was caught filling one of my wellington boots with cheese sandwiches and jelly—secondhand if you get my drift.

IF OUR CHILD IS HANGING
OUT WITH OTHER KIDS
THAT TEST OUR
TOLERANCE,
IT'S A GOOD THING.

## Your Role as a Child

So, you're a grown-up now and probably don't recognize yourself as a child. But you are still a child, although you'll get strange looks if you park in a "parents with children" space if you happen to go shopping with your mother or father.

Until both of your parents are passed on and you have been promoted, so to speak, you remain a child. And you have a responsibility. You have a duty—now you are a Rules Player—to be courteous, thoughtful, patient, and cooperative toward your parents.

Yes, yes, I know they drive you mad, but from now on you have a role and it is simply this:

- To behave impeccably with them
- To look after them if that's what they want/need
- To back off if that's what they want/need
- To listen to them when they chatter on, without losing your patience or sighing
- To appreciate that they have had a long and hard life and gathered a lot of experience—some of which may be of some use to you—and you won't know if you carry on shaking your head and ignoring everything they say
- To visit, write, phone, communicate more often than you think you should—but probably not as much as they think you should
- Not to bad mouth them in front of your children but to talk them up as being the greatest grandparents in the world

- To be pleased when they come to stay and happily let them watch whatever TV program they want without complaining

And why will you do all this? Because they gave you life, brought you up. Yes, yes, I know they made mistakes along the way but you forgive them all of them (see Rule 70) and you turned out fine. Oh yes you did.

Parents deserve decent treatment when they get old and need attention and someone to listen to them and take them seriously—and they make great baby/dog sitters (and usually free as well).

> YOU HAVE A DUTY
> TO BE COURTEOUS,
> THOUGHTFUL, AND
> COOPERATIVE TOWARD
> YOUR PARENTS.

# Your Role as a Parent

Gosh, this is a tough one. You have a role and it is important, but how do we define it, make it real for you, so that you can live by it, put it into practice?

If you are crazy enough to take on the role of parent, then you are signing an invisible contract with your children to give and get them the very best of everything you can. And I don't necessarily mean material possessions. Your mission, should you choose to accept it, is to be all that the very best parenting requires. You will be encouraging, supportive, kind, patient, educational, loyal, honest, caring, and loving.

You will have to make sure they eat the best food for developing children. You will supply them with the best education for their talents and skills. You will aim to develop their interests in all areas and not just the ones you are keen on. You will set clear boundaries so they know what's what, and what they can and can't do—and with clear and acceptable levels of discipline should they overstep the mark. You will adjust your degree of supervision to match their age—little ones need closer supervision than big ones. You will always provide a safe haven for them to come home to—no matter how much trouble they've got themselves into in the big bad world outside.

You will be firm, loving, sharing, caring, and responsible. You will set them standards and be a role model to them. You won't do or say anything you wouldn't be proud of them knowing. You will stand up for them, protect them, and keep them safe.

You will stretch their imaginations and feed them with stimuli so they grow up creative, excited about the world, and raring to go.

You will approve of them, boost their self-esteem, improve their confidence, and send them out into the world literate, educated, polite, helpful, and productive members of society. And when the time comes for them to leave the nest, you will help them pack and keep giving that support while they find their feet (or should that be wings?).

Not much then, really.

YOUR MISSION,
SHOULD YOU CHOOSE
TO ACCEPT IT,
IS TO BE ALL THAT THE
VERY BEST PARENTING
REQUIRES.

PART IV

SOCIAL
RULES

Every day we come into contact with real live human beings—at work, commuting, in shops, out and about—people we might have met before or often complete strangers. The world is full of people with whom we interact. Those interactions, small or large, can be life-affirming or deeply unpleasant. So, what follows are a few social Rules. These aren't set in stone. They aren't a revelation. They are a reminder.

We will look at some Rules for dealing with people at work. After all, that's where we spend an awful lot of our time, and anything we can do to make our career more successful and our working life happier, more satisfying and productive, and most of all enjoyable, surely can't be a bad thing?

Social Rules are the fourth circle we draw around ourselves. (The first is self, the second is partner, the third is family and friends, and the fourth is social relationships.) It's terribly easy to see our own group, social class, or any level of community as the right one, the important one, the better-than-yours one. But each community sees itself as that. How much better to draw that fourth circle around ourselves so that it includes people from other backgrounds, other ethnicities, other communities, so that we feel part of the big community, the human one. It is better to include more than to exclude even one. And it is very easy to exclude for whatever reason, to assume that it is a "them" and "us" situation, when actually we are all "them," we are all "us."

We have to treat everyone with respect, or what's it all about? We have to care about everyone, or the whole thing falls apart. We have to help each other no matter who they are, because if we don't there won't be anyone to help us when we need it. We have to be the first to put our hand out. Why? Because we are Rules Players.

# RULE 87

## We're All Closer Than You Think

I have a friend. Not a good friend particularly, more of an acquaintance. He's a regular sort of a guy. Runs a computer business. Has a family. Normal, regular, 9 to 5, straight, nothing unusual about him. Or so he thought.

He is English, born and bred. He used to have a bit of a rant about immigration. Went on a bit about numbers, but you always felt it was a bit deeper than that. He found out not long back that he was actually adopted. Nothing wrong with that—plenty are—but it set him to tracing his family. Yep, you've guessed it. His father was a foreigner.* Now you wouldn't know it to look at the man, but he's only half as English as he thought he was. Interesting.

If you trace back anyone's history, it's going to throw up a lot of different bits from different communities and ethnic groupings. None of us is in any way "pure." The whole thing has been melted, shaken and stirred, and blended until any one of us would be hard-pressed to swear where we originated. Go back far enough, and we all contain something a bit different. Apparently half of all European males carry a line that can be traced back to Genghis Khan—and he came from Mongolia.

My point? Don't judge others, because we are all human, all drawn from the same melting pot. We are all related if you go back far enough. There is no difference. We have to accept other communities, other cultures even if they are very different from ours because the difference between us is so very little when you wipe away the veneer we all wear.

*That's his word, by the way, not mine.

Yes, we may wear different clothes and speak different languages and have different customs, but we all fall in love, all want someone to hold and hug, to have a family, to be happy and successful, not to be afraid of the dark, to live a long time, die a good death, to be attractive and not to get fat, old, or sick. What does it matter if we wear a suit, a sari, or a grass skirt if deep down we all cry when we are hurt, we laugh when we are joyful, and our stomachs rumble when we are hungry? The veneer can be wiped away in a second, and then we are all the same, all quite lovely and quite, quite human.

THE DIFFERENCE
BETWEEN US IS
SO VERY LITTLE WHEN YOU
WIPE AWAY THE VENEER
WE ALL WEAR.

# RULE 88

## It Doesn't Hurt to Forgive

It's easy to be angry. It's easy to get riled up and mutter or to make rude gestures and swear. It isn't so easy to be forgiving. And I'm not talking about turning the other cheek here or any of that stuff. I'm talking about seeing it from the other person's point of view. And being forgiving.

I had an incident recently on vacation that basically involved a very wet cyclist mouthing off because he thought someone (no, it wasn't me) had driven too close to him and nearly forced him into a ditch. He was loud, rude, aggressive, out of order, and foul-mouthed. I tried to speak to him reasonably on behalf of the person he was being abusive to, and he gave me a mouthful as well. Then he rode off and shook his fist at me, which made his bicycle wobble and inside I laughed, a lot. I found it easy to forgive him not in any religious sense but because I could see he had chosen the wrong vacation.

He had obviously been persuaded that the cycling vacation would be fun, but it was in hilly, really hilly, countryside, and it had rained all that day. He was tired, wet, aching, and very unhappy. How could I not forgive him? If I had foolishly chosen that vacation, I too would have been grumpy, ready for a fight, fed up, touchy, and raw. I felt quite sorry for him and could sense a great deal of his unhappiness. Yes, he was in the wrong to use such foul language—especially in front of children. Yes, he was ready for a fight and intimidating and aggressive. But he was also me or you or anyone else in that situation—cold, wet, miserable. And who is to say we would-n't have lost our temper if we, too, had chosen the wrong vacation?

Being forgiving doesn't mean we have to be pushed around or to put up with nonsense. We can stand our ground and say, "Sorry I don't need to take that," but we can also make an attempt to forgive because we can see it from their point of view. Maybe the word is tolerant rather than forgiving. But either way, we don't have to mistake forgiveness or tolerance or whatever with meekness. We can still be saying, "Shove off with your bad language and sad bicycle and your mother smells of hamsters," while feeling sorry for the poor idiot at the same time. He was a good man who did a naughty thing.

Just bear in mind that anyone you come into contact with who makes you angry may have had a really bad time before getting to you.

> BEING FORGIVING
> DOESN'T MEAN WE
> HAVE TO BE
> PUSHED AROUND.

# RULE 89

# It Doesn't Hurt to Be Helpful

We said in the previous Rule that the angry person you encounter may have had a bad day before getting to you. Let's try to make it a good day for all of them before they get to someone else. Let's spread a bit of goodwill around out there and then maybe, just maybe, mad cyclists won't be quite so ready to rear up and be abusive and aggressive. Perhaps no one had been kind to him that day. Perhaps no one had been kind to him for a very long time. See, it's all your fault. If only you'd been a bit nicer to him, he wouldn't have taken out his wet angst on the rest of us that day.

Always offering a hand and being generally decent to every-body is really easy once we get into the mindset that it's what we are supposed to be doing. It can become your "default" behavior. So your first reaction becomes, "Yes, sure, I can show you how to do that, no problem," rather than, "I'm very busy; can't you ask someone else?"

Try it as a different approach at work and see what it does for your reputation and career. Being known as someone who is always ready to help does not get you known as a pushover. Quite the reverse, in fact.

If you see a woman in trouble—even if it's only that they've spilled their groceries getting it into the back of the car—you can always go up and say, "Can I help?" If she wants you to she'll accept and if not…well, you tried, and that's the main thing.

This is all about going into every day thinking the best of people, being the first to smile, seeing where somebody might need a hand instead of bustling on past. It's about trying to see a situation from others' viewpoint, being sympathetic if they have problems—you don't have to solve them all. It means taking the time and trouble to make sure people around you are OK. And yes, this does mean strangers as well. If we all took the trouble to smile occasionally at strangers, the world might start each day on a slightly less confrontational foot.

THIS IS ALL ABOUT GOING INTO EVERY DAY THINKING THE BEST OF PEOPLE.

# RULE 90

## What's in It for Them?

We all want to win. At work and in most aspects of life, winning is good, and we don't like to lose. No one sets out to be a loser. But we do tend to think that if we are going to win then someone else, someone around us, has to lose. But it doesn't have to be that way.

In every situation, the smart Rules Player weighs up the circumstances and asks, "What's in it for them?" If you know what's motivating others, you can help steer the situation (and your actions) so you get what you want, but they feel they've gotten something out of it, too. The "win-win" mentality might have come out of the workplace, but it applies to pretty much every situation and relationship.

To work out what others are likely to want and need, take a step back and remain a little detached, so you're looking at the situation as if from outside. Suddenly it stops being you and them, and you'll stop thinking that they need to give way in order for you to win.

Dealing with somebody who's got the hang of this Rule is a rewarding experience—people will look forward to working with you, because there's an air of cooperation and understanding. Once you've learned to always look for the other person's "bottom line," you'll become very fluid in your negotiations and will gain a reputation for being adult and supportive—and that's another bit of winning for you as well.

And it's not just in workplace negotiations that this win-win reaps rewards. Try it at home, too. If you're debating where to go on vacation, and you desperately want to go horseback riding in France, think "what's in it for them?"—what is it about that vacation that will make them happy? Highlight those aspects, and they're more likely to agree. If you're struggling to think of anything that will appeal to them, you need to think more broadly—maybe you can find a place where you go horseback riding while they go fishing or sailing. You see how it works. Just asking the question, "what's in it for them?" helps you think it through.

Being a parent is another area where this works. If you just lay down the law without considering what your children want and need, they'll rebel or at least be difficult to handle. But again ask "What's in it for them?," and you'll see the situation from their perspective and handle it better. Winner.

YOU GET WHAT YOU WANT, BUT THEY FEEL THEY'VE GOTTEN SOMETHING OUT OF IT, TOO.

# Hang Out with Positive People

If you want to be successful in your life, at work, socializing, you need to be aware that there are two groups of people to hang out with. First, there are those who lift you up, are positive about life, have energy and enthusiasm, walk their walk, talk their walk, and generally make you feel great to be alive. And then there are the moaners who bring you down to their level of inactivity. The second group are not the group to hang out with if you want to make things happen and be happy.

So hang out with the positive, smart people. I mean people who feel life is an exciting challenge worth wrestling to the ground and having fun with. The sort of people who have interesting points of view, who make you feel good talking to them, who have positive things to say or suggest rather than moaning. The sort of people who tell you that you look fantastic rather than criticize you.

Earlier on we talked about clearing clutter out of your life— physical stuff (see Rule 39). Now maybe it is time to clear some people clutter. (Hmm that sounds terribly LA*.) Let's have a look at the people you do hang out with.

Which ones can you honestly say make you:

- Feel enthusiastic about seeing them?
- Rise to every challenge?
- Laugh and smile and feel great about yourself?
- Feel supported and nurtured and encouraged?
- Feel stimulate you with new ideas, new concepts, and new directions?

* If this book is on sale in LA, then I meant somewhere else entirely.

And which ones make you:

- Feel depressed after you've seen them?
- Feel angry, dejected, or criticized?
- Squash your ideas and pour cold water on your plans?
- Feel you're not taken seriously?
- Feel as if you can't achieve anything?

Hang out with the first group. Cull the second group—unless they are just having a bad day (and we all have those). Move on, get it done. Ah, but you'll say it is cruel to prune friends ruthlessly like that. Well, I suppose it is, but then I want to enjoy my friends, not moan about them. If I find myself doing that, I prune them. No point hanging out with people who don't make you feel good—not unless you like being down.

NO POINT HANGING OUT
WITH PEOPLE WHO DON'T
MAKE YOU FEEL GOOD.

# RULE 92

## Be Generous with Your Time and Information

As you get older—and probably not any wiser (see Rule 2)—you will learn a lot of stuff. Some of that stuff will be important to other people, often younger people, but not always. Share what you know with them. Don't hold on to information for the sake of it. Don't hold on to your time for the sake of it. What would you be doing with it that could be in any way more worthwhile?

If you have a special talent or skill, pass it on. I don't necessarily mean you have to spend all your spare evenings down at the local youth club teaching young punks all about whatever it is you do or know about.

But if the opportunity arises, then go for it. I was recently asked to give a talk to a bunch of 6 year olds about what it means to be an author. At first I thought, "But I'm not an author; I might just qualify, and only just, as a writer." But an author sounded far too grand, too fictitious, too grown-up for me. What on earth could I tell 6-year-olds about what I do for a living? But, remembering my own Rule, I warmly and graciously accepted and went along. I must say I had one of the most pleasurable mornings in a long time. They were fantastic. They asked brilliant questions, paid attention, chatted in a very adult way, were keen and interested, and in general were well behaved and marvelous. It would have been so easy to say no. And you never know what you might inspire in others, what flame you might fan, what encouragement you might give without even knowing.

This Rule especially applies at work. It's very easy to fall into the mindset that if you know stuff that nobody else does, then you have the upper hand–to believe that knowledge is power and you should hang on to every little bit of it. Actually, the most successful people in life are always looking to pass on what they know, to bring on others in their wake. Because if you don't, then who's going to replace you? You make yourself indispensable, and you have just wedged yourself in a career rut.

If you're not passing on your talents and skills; what are you doing with them? What great secrets have you got that demand to be withheld from the world? Or is it laziness? Successful Rules Players say yes as often as possible because there is an incredible experience to be had in passing stuff on. And it is genuinely useful. Don't go thinking that what you know is of no use to anyone. I guarantee it will be quite the opposite, because the second you say yes, you become one step up from all those who say no. That makes you important, successful, decisive, and generous. And that makes you special.

IF YOU HAVE A SPECIAL
TALENT OR SKILL,
PASS IT ON.

# RULE 93

## Get Involved

Get involved in what? Anything really (or at least almost anything). I guess what I mean by this is to take an interest in your world. Don't watch it on television, but go out there and interact with it. Too many people are living their lives through the lives of others seen on that little screen. Or even living their life vicariously through the lives of others in the real world. (Gossip keeps them going.) There is a great big wide world out there full of life, vitality, energy, experience, drive, excitement. Getting involved means get out there and be part of it. Get out there and find out what it all means and how it works. Watching TV is warm and safe and comfortable. Being out there can be scary, cold, uncomfortable. But at least you know you're alive.

People are always complaining that life goes faster as they get older. But my experience is that the more we do out in the world, the more time seems to be stretched. If we watch TV, whole evenings can vanish before our very eyes.

Getting involved means cooperating, contributing, taking part. Not watching from the sidelines while someone else has your life for you. Getting involved means rolling up your sleeves and getting your hands dirty but having an experience along the way, a real experience. Getting involved means joining in, offering help, volunteering, turning a theoretical interest into a real one, being out there and talking to people. Getting involved means having fun—real fun, not TV fun. Getting involved means helping other people appreciate and enjoy their lives a bit more than they would have done without you.

I have noticed that successful people—and that is what this book is all about, and by successful I do mean content and happy rather than wealthy or famous—have outside interests that don't earn them any money or bring them any kudos. Stuff they do for the fun of it, to be helpful, to encourage others. They often find the time by doing it instead of watching more TV (seriously).

They become volunteers, mentors, school governors, local business advisers, charity workers. They join groups, associations, clubs, societies. They get out there and belong and have fun. They put themselves out there to make a difference or share an interest. They go to evening classes in ridiculous subjects. Maybe they laugh and poke gentle fun at themselves for doing it. Maybe they even sometimes wish they hadn't gotten involved because some things can creep up and take over your life. But they are part of something. Part of the world—in a full and proper sense.

GETTING INVOLVED MEANS ROLLING UP YOUR SLEEVES AND GETTING YOUR HANDS DIRTY BUT HAVING A REAL EXPERIENCE ALONG THE WAY.

## Keep the Moral High Ground

Boy, is this a simple one to say and a really difficult one to live up to. I do appreciate that it's a tough one, but I know you can do it. It takes a simple shift of vision, from being the sort of person who acts in a certain way to being a different sort of person who acts in a different sort of way. Look, no matter how rough it gets, you are never going to:

- Take revenge
- Act badly
- Be very, very angry
- Hurt anyone
- Act without thinking
- Act rashly
- Be aggressive

That's it, the bottom line. You are going to maintain the moral high ground at all times. You are going to behave honestly, decently, kindly, forgivingly, nicely (whatever that means) no matter what the provocation. No matter what the challenge thrown at you. No matter how unfairly others behave. No matter how badly they behave. You will not retaliate in like kind. You will carry on being good and civilized and morally irreproachable. Your manners will be impeccable. Your language moderated and dignified. There is nothing others can do or say that will make you deviate from this line.

Yes, I know it's difficult at times. I know when the rest of the world is behaving appallingly, and you have to carry on taking it on the chin without giving in to your desire to floor someone with a savage word, it's really, really tough. When people are being horrid to you, it's natural to want to get your own back and lash out. Don't. Once this rough time has passed, you will be so proud of yourself for keeping the moral high ground that it will taste a thousand times better than revenge ever would.

I know revenge is tempting, but you won't go there. Not now, not ever. Why? Because if you do you'll be sinking to others' level, you'll be at one with the beasts instead of the angels (see Rule 9), because it demeans you and cheapens you, because you will regret it, and lastly because if you do, then you're no Rules Player. Revenge is for losers. Taking and keeping the moral high ground is the only way to be. It doesn't mean you're a pushover or a wimp. It just means that any action you do take will be honest and dignified and clean.

KEEPING THE MORAL HIGH GROUND WILL TASTE A THOUSAND TIMES BETTER THAN REVENGE EVER WOULD.

## Just Because You Have, Doesn't Mean They Have, Too

I was at school with a guy whose family had relatively little money when he was growing up. Actually, compared to many people in the world, he really wasn't that badly off. But compared to most of the other kids in school, he had less. This is partly what drove him to get a high-powered city job eventually, and he is now very comfortably off. Probably better off than most of the people he was at school with. But boy does he have a chip on his shoulder about money. He hugely resents anyone having money they haven't worked as hard for as he has, and he makes cutting remarks to friends, such as, "It's nice that you can afford to go to the Bahamas for a month on vacation. Not everyone can, you know." That's certainly true, but he can.

Look, everyone has troubles to cope with, now and in the past. You can't give other people a hard time just because they haven't suffered like you have. Whether you had a rotten childhood, are poor, have a relationship that doesn't make you happy, didn't get the job you wanted, or can't have a dog because you're allergic—whether your troubles are big or small, the point is that it's not their fault. You have no idea what else your friends have had to contend with in their lives, or will so in the future. They may not have it any easier than you on balance.

If you go round trying to make your friends feel guilty about having some things easy or good, you'll just end up damaging your friendships. Then are you going to go round resenting people with more friends than you? No, I know you wouldn't do that—but some would. And what's the alternative? Would you wish a miserable childhood or poverty or a bad marriage or redundancy or a dog hair allergy on your friends? I certainly hope not. If you're living your life the best you can, you'll want to see as many other people happy as possible. So you should be pleased every time you encounter someone who didn't have it rough.

I don't want to be unsympathetic to people with tough lives. Of course I'm not. But by becoming bitter, you make your life even worse. Just be happy for other people if they don't have the crosses to bear that you did or do.

That friend of mine, by the way, may have been born into a relatively poor family, but he was born with brains. That's how come he got into Oxford University and a plum city job. But does he feel guilty toward all those people who weren't born as clever as him? Of course he doesn't. But I bet there are people with chips on their shoulders about the fact that he went to a top college and they didn't. Gosh, what a lot of wasted resentment there is in the world. Let's do our bit by not adding to it.

> BY BECOMING BITTER,
> YOU MAKE YOUR LIFE
> EVEN WORSE.

# RULE 96

## Do Compare Yourself with Other People

This isn't the original version of this book, you know.* In the first edition (as in this one, I invited readers to email me their own Rules. This particular one—which I couldn't agree with more—was suggested to me by a 16-year-old schoolboy from India. I mention this for two reasons. First, because it just goes to show that you're never too young to follow the Rules. And second, because I think it's significant that this comes from someone who is still in education and therefore expects to learn from other people. It's a Rule that demands a measure of humility that all of us could do with (well, alright then, I could do with).

People often tell us not to compare ourselves with others. The argument for this is that it's arrogant if we think we're better, and demoralizing if we think we're worse. Also that we're all different, so the comparison can't be accurate. However, when you're at work, you're constantly set targets for performance, and quite right, too. And, in fact, we should set our own targets in our personal lives, as per Rule 29. And this applies not only to our plans, but also to our own behavior and development.

None of us is perfect—we all know that. We all wish we could be more patient or kinder or more tolerant or harder working or better parents or more sensible with money. But how much more? The best way to decide where to aim is to use someone you respect as a touchstone. "I'd like to be as well organized as this person" or "as calm as that person." You see? You're comparing yourself to other people, but in a positive way. It means

---

*Don't worry, you're not missing out. This version is bigger and better.

you can see how much work you have to do, and you can see that it's achievable. You don't have to tell them you're using them as your guide, although you can certainly ask their advice if it would help.

You might think that it could be depressing always to be comparing yourself with people who are better than you. But as my 16-year-old friend wisely points out, one is good and the other is better. No one is scoring badly here, and anyway you get extra brownie points for the fact that you're being honest with yourself about where there's room to improve and then taking positive steps to do it.

Seeing the people around us as teachers is something that comes naturally when you're 16. Sadly, we can lose that attitude as we get older. But if we have any sense, we surround ourselves with good, positive people, so actually it would be odd if we couldn't learn from them, wouldn't it? And it's our best chance of beating Rule 2.**

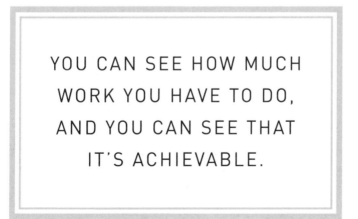

YOU CAN SEE HOW MUCH
WORK YOU HAVE TO DO,
AND YOU CAN SEE THAT
IT'S ACHIEVABLE.

**You mean you haven't learned them by heart? Rule 2 is "You'll Get Older but Not Necessarily Wiser."

# RULE 97

## Have a Plan for Your Career

So where are you going at work? Have you a plan? A goal? Even a humble aim? If you don't have any of these, chances are you're going to drift. If you have a plan, you stand a better chance of getting to where you want to be. Knowing where you want to be is 90 percent of the battle. Knowing where you want to be means you've sat down and thought about things, that you've been conscious about your future and have focused your attention on it.

Once you've looked ahead and decided where you want to be—and there is no right or wrong about where that is, you can be as determined and ambitious as you want—you can plan the logical steps you need to get you there. And once you have those steps, you can work out what you need to do to make each a reality. Is it further qualifications? Experience? To change jobs? To change the way you work? Whatever it takes for you to make those steps is what you have to do. Don't stagnate. Don't get stuck in a rut.

We all need to work to earn a living. Staying at home watching daytime TV really isn't an option. Work keeps your mind fit and active as well as gets you in touch with other people, and work presents a daily challenge. Believe you me, we are better off with it than without it.

If you don't have a plan, you could end up anywhere. Yes, sure, that might be exciting, but I doubt that many people end up happy and successful merely by chance. It's something you have to work at, consciously. And having a plan is part of that conscious effort. I know luck plays a crucial part in some people's lives, but only a very few. And formulating a plan and working hard while you're waiting for the luck to turn up doesn't mean that it won't, or that when it does you aren't free to throw away the plan completely.

If you're not busy planning and working toward the next goal, there is a real chance you can fall into a downward spiral of despondency and apathy. Successful people have "get up and go"—and when they don't have it naturally, they artificially create it. They pretend to if you like, but the very act of pretending gets them up and about. Try it; it works.

STAYING AT HOME
WATCHING DAYTIME TV
REALLY ISN'T
AN OPTION.

# RULE 98

## Look at the Long-Term Ramifications of What You Do for a Living

Just as your community has an effect, so, too, does what you do for a living. It is no longer safe or responsible or ethical to carry on working without thinking about what we do and the effect it has. I'm not going to question you about what it is you do. That is entirely for you to do. As a writer, I am aware that a lot of good trees could die young because of me. Balanced against that are the positive effects (I hope) of what I write, and people who are employed as a result of the writing. Ah, but I have no control over their working conditions, so I'm off the hook there. Or am I?

So, for me it is dead trees, the electricity I use in my office, and the pollution caused by trucks delivering books to book-stores, to name but a few by-products of my sitting here tapping away. What about you? Handled any hazardous waste lately? Or designed a missile guidance system? Or logged an entire rain forest? Or does your work provide an essential service or product; does it make people happier, wealthier, or more successful?

What we do for a living has an impact. We can be working in an industry that pollutes, causes harm, is unpleasant and bad. Or we might be working to help others, to benefit people posi-tively. Knowing that what we do causes an effect—for good or bad—doesn't mean we have to instantly chuck everything up and change jobs. Nor does it mean we can sit back and relax and think we're doing OK just because we work in a caring job.

Every job, every industry has some ramifications—good and bad. Everything we do at work can have great benefit or cause harm. We have to weigh it all up and check how we feel about it. And if we are unhappy we can leave, but not too fast because there's a great chance we can change things from the inside.

I worked in one industry for a while where I was aware that things were a bit dodgy, so I adopted the line of asking, "What if the press got hold of this, what would that do to us?" I wasn't whistle-blowing or opposing anyone, merely asking. But it did draw attention to the fact that what was happening was slightly the other side of a fine line. Maybe you could do the same. Or maybe you can slowly, quietly use the influence that you have and the actions you are able to take to change things ever so slightly for the better.

AS A WRITER, I AM AWARE
THAT A LOT OF GOOD
TREES COULD DIE YOUNG
BECAUSE OF ME.

# RULE 99

## Be Good at Your Job

How we behave at work has an effect on our colleagues. We need to have standards—and stick to them, of course. We have to be moral and decent and honest and trustworthy, of course. But here are a few others to help you become fantastically successful along the way.

- Treat your job as important and do it to the very best of your ability. Don't stand still but learn all the time. Stay ahead of your industry and new developments.

- Always be on the lookout for ways to improve the lot of everyone rather than just yourself. Think in terms of "we" rather than "I." You are a part of a team and should fit in and be a part effectively and efficiently.

- Try to spread a little happiness as you go. Don't badmouth people. Stick up for the underdog. Compliment people and be genuine about it. Don't indulge in gossip. Keep your own counsel, and be a bit aloof. It'll get you promoted.

- Dress smartly, and try to make a good impression. Maintain high standards, and put in the hours. Try not to go to work to sleep or steal the pens or look for love. You are there to work; get on with it.

- Try to be kind to colleagues; they are as lost as you once were. Give them a break, a chance, a bit of slack. Encourage them by example. Be a role model for junior members of staff. Try to understand your boss's point of view and to see things from the company perspective.

- Understand the politics of office life—and don't get involved of course—but use it to your own advantage. Don't be frightened to put yourself forward or to volunteer (just so long as you know what you are volunteering for). There is no kudos in being work-shy. Be proud of being effective and efficient.

- Know your boundaries. Know how to say "no," and mean it. Don't let anyone take advantage of your good nature. Be assertive without being aggressive.

- Enjoy what you do. Have a passion for your work. Have fun.

WE HAVE TO BE MORAL
AND DECENT AND HONEST
AND TRUSTWORTHY,
OF COURSE.

# RULE 100

## Be Aware of the Damage You Are Doing

This Rule doesn't mean, as yet, that you have to do anything. All it means is a conscious decision to evaluate what you are doing to the environment, the world, and whether it is a good thing or a bad thing. You might choose to change what you do in the light of this evaluation. Or you may not, either because you figure what the heck or because you figure you're pretty "green" already and don't need to change anything.

The reason I say "Don't do anything as yet" is that it is all too easy to rush headlong into action without having all the facts in front of you. You need to know if the changes you are making are actually making things better or worse. For example, when my youngest child was born, I was seriously concerned about the reports of the damage disposable diapers were doing. Apparently, they take some 500 years to decompose. But I was also concerned that cloth diapers took a lot of washing with all the usage of electricity, soap, water, etc. And some argue they are both as bad as each other when it comes to damaging the environment. Trouble is, you have to use something, or you risk damaging your carpets…

So you might like to consider what car you drive; what sort of heating you use in your house; how you get to your vacation destinations (planes aren't that environmentally friendly by all accounts); whether you recycle; if somebody else can use what you don't want—that sort of thing. I leave the details entirely up to you (heaven forbid that I should lecture anyone on these matters) but it's good to have a conscience about these things and to try to minimize the damage we are doing.

This goes back to the big theme underpinning all of the Rules, namely that we need to go through our lives with our eyes open, conscious and aware of what we are doing and the effect we are having on the environment and on other people around us. We don't have to become goody-goodies, but we should be at least giving it some thought.

I think the time for complacency is over, and it really is time to consider the impact we make quite carefully. And once we have considered it, we might like to start making a few changes to improve things. If we all did a little bit, it would make a grand difference.

WE DON'T HAVE TO
BECOME GOODY-GOODIES,
BUT WE SHOULD BE AT
LEAST GIVING IT SOME
THOUGHT.

# RULE 101

## Be for the Glory, Not the Degradation

We can work for the glory of humankind, or we can try to bring it all crashing down into degradation. Shakespeare is for the glory; a crack house is for the degradation. A neighborhood party on a warm summer's afternoon is for the glory; stealing someone's purse is for the degradation. And it doesn't have to be tame; a parachute jump for charity is for the glory; porn is for the degradation—but an erotic movie can be for the glory. Get the idea?

Anything that makes us more than we are, makes us strive for perfection, improves us, challenges us, excites us in a good way, makes us rise above our base nature, and brings us out into the sunshine is for the glory.

So what are you going to be for? The glory or the degradation? Well, for the glory, of course. My fear is that you will think this is all about being good and that has a bad press. All our lives we have been told that being good is a bad thing, somehow dull, for the meek and goody-goodies, the sandal wearers, the holier-than-thou brigade. Being good hasn't had a lot going for it. As a kid at school, if you tried to be good, you got beaten up. At work if you try to be good they call you the boss's pet.

Well, being good, being for the glory is a private thing. You don't have to tell a soul. If you keep it quiet, you are being good. If you brag about it, you are a goody-goody. If you interfere with others and try to make them be good, you are a do-gooder. Just make a decision to be for the glory and say nothing.

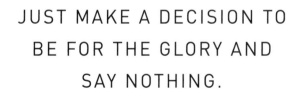

JUST MAKE A DECISION TO BE FOR THE GLORY AND SAY NOTHING.

# Be Part of the Solution, Not the Problem

This goes further than just being good, being for glory not degradation. This is about positive, affirmative action. Look, if we don't take some action then this world, this fabulous planet of ours, is going to hell in a handbasket. I was reading an article the other day about the Easter Islands and how they could stand as a perfect metaphor for our own sad predicament.

The Easter Islands were settled by a Polynesian race around 500 years ago.* They found an island heavy with wildlife and heavily wooded with trees. Within a few short years, they had eaten the way through the wildlife and chopped down all the trees. They also polluted the rivers and were on the verge of extinction. The only thing that has rescued them is tourism.

Planet Earth has no tourists. No one is going to rescue us so they can take our photo. We all have to start being a part of the solution now and stop adding to the mayhem, the destruction, the problem. And we start to be part of the solution when we stand up and get counted. We stop the problem when we stop saying, "I was just doing my duty," or "It was part of my job." Come on, we have to stop the nonsense now, or we're going to be relegated to being some vast amusement park for aliens—who aren't coming.

*Don't write in if I got the facts vaguely wrong—it's a metaphor.

So the Rule is to start looking for ways we can personally contribute to the solution. We have to take part, get involved, find solutions, take action, get off our backsides and contribute. If you want your life to feel right, to be good, to be successful and mean something, you have to put something back. You have to pay back your loan. You have to reinvest in life, and that means caring and wanting things to get better.

LOOK, IF WE DON'T TAKE
SOME ACTION
THEN THIS WORLD,
THIS FABULOUS PLANET
OF OURS,
IS GOING TO HELL IN A
HANDBASKET.

# RULE 103

## Check What History Would Say About You

So what is history going to say about you? What do you feel in your heart of hearts is going to be your epithet after you've gone? And I don't mean what is engraved on your tombstone but written in some great cosmic record of the universe. Personally, I don't think I'll even warrant a footnote. But if I do, I would like history to record that I had a go, made an effort, tried my best to make a difference. That I stood up for what I believed in, stood up to get counted, and stood up for my rights. I would like history to say, maybe, that I got up off my backside and just stood up—it would be enough.

And you, my friend, what would you like? What do you think history will say? What would you like history to say? Is there a gap between these two? Can you bridge it? What do you have to do to make that gap connect? Think about both what it would say about you as a person and about your deeds.

We have to care, if we want to be successful, that those who come after are going to inherit a better world than the one we found ourselves in. You remember all those books on self-sufficiency that were all the rage back in the 1970s?* Well, a key thing they all seemed to have in common was they said if you had land, you had to make better use of it than the person who had it before you. You had to improve it. Same with this world. We have to consciously make the effort to improve it before we go. We have to take responsibility for what we've been given and make a better use of it before we shuffle off and pass it on.

* Yes, yes, I, too, was sold the dream and moved to the country to grow my own yogurt, wear sandals, and eat lentils. It didn't last long—not for me anyway.

How will we point at the polluted oceans, the dried-up rivers, the melted ice caps and say to our metaphorical children, "One day all this will be yours—oh, and sorry about what we did with it." I think they may be a little angry at us. History may indeed write us off as termite people. We have destroyed and polluted and slaughtered and made a pretty poor show of things. Individually, we can make a difference. We must make a difference. Individually history must hold us accountable.

The trouble is there are so many people who won't change because they think they won't be held accountable. If there is no one watching, they think they can get away with murder. History will make short work of them.

> HISTORY MAY INDEED
> WRITE US OFF AS
> TERMITE PEOPLE.

## Not Everything Can Be Green

I've just heard about a man* who invented shoes that recharge your mobile phone battery while you're walking. Brilliant. I want a pair, but they all look like rugged walking boots—designed for areas where recharging equipment isn't available, such as jungles and deserts. I'll have a pair when they make them in Oxford brogues. Not everything can be green. Not everyone can be as organic and as green as we would have them be.

OK, we've gone through the rant about the state of the world and what we're doing to it. Now I'm going to give you a tiny get-out clause. Not everything can be green. There has to be by-products. There has to be some pollution. There has to be some damage. We are vast in number—billions of humans living on the planet have to have an effect—and we have to live. There will always be some damage. Our job is to limit it, but it is unrealistic to attempt to eliminate it altogether. It's all a question of balance, of priorities.

It is unrealistic to demand the immediate elimination of all motor vehicles in the world; it's not going to happen. But we can do our bit by buying cars that use less fuel, emit cleaner exhaust fumes, use recyclable materials in their construction. But they won't be totally green. They can't be.

We might all rush off to disaster zones to lend a hand, but we'll fly there, and aircraft emit huge quantities of exhaust fumes. You see, we are making choices all the time. Driving to work, heating our homes, what we wear, what we eat. We can't

---

*Trevor Bayliss—he also invented the wind-up radio.

expect everyone to be as green as we want to be. We can't expect everything to be as green as we would have it.

If we all manage to achieve a reduction, it helps. If we all do our bit, it helps. If we are all conscious about what we are doing, it helps. But we can't expect perfection. We can't turn things around overnight. If you're trying so hard to be green that it's causing you a great deal of stress and your life is suffering as a result (just try to go food/household shopping and buy nothing at all in plastic, and you'll quickly see what I mean), then stop. Make an effort, but accept that it's never going to be totally perfect. Just so long as we are trying to do something, it helps.

NOT EVERYONE CAN BE AS ORGANIC AND AS GREEN AS WE WOULD HAVE THEM BE.

# RULE 105

## Put Something Back

I firmly believe that none of us asked to be born and that this world doesn't owe us a living, or anything. But by the same token we are in debt up to our armpits. Sure, we didn't get a choice about being here, but once we are here we get fed and watered, entertained and amused, challenged and educated, awed and flabbergasted. It's all here on offer for us. We can do pretty much anything we want. We can take from this world all it has to offer. And this world has an amazing amount to offer all of us.

We can take and take and take. There is nothing to say we can't. What I am suggesting is that we sleep better at night if we put something back. After the show, be one of the volunteers clearing up.

Be generous with everything. Be generous with your generosity. You don't have to give money, but rather your time and care. If you have a special talent, use it to help others in some way. If you have facilities, lend them to others who need them. If you have the power to effect change for the better, then use it. If you have influence, use it.

And if you don't? I'm sure that we all can make a difference in our own small way. We might have to look carefully or use our imagination a bit or be creative in how we define "giving something back."

We don't all have to become charity workers or missionaries, but we could sponsor a child in need. We don't have to turn our house into a shelter for the homeless, but we could start a wildlife patch in our garden. We don't have to become totally organic, but we could recycle a bit more or just ask questions about the companies we choose to buy from.

I guess we all have to ask ourselves: "Is this world a richer place for me being in it? Will I leave it a better place than when I came into it? Have I made a difference to someone's life? Have I put something back?"

WE SLEEP BETTER
AT NIGHT IF WE PUT
SOMETHING BACK.

# RULE 106

## Find a New Rule Every Day—or Occasionally at Least

So, that's about it—106 Rules for a successful and fulfilled life. Phew. But don't think it's over yet. There is no time to sit still; there are no coffee breaks for Rules Players. As soon as you think you've got it handled, you'll fall flat on your face. You have to keep moving forward. You have to be inventive, creative, imaginative, resourceful, original. This final Rule has to be to keep thinking up new Rules, not to stand still, to carry on developing this theme, adding to, improving on, evolving and growing and changing these Rules. These provide a jumping-off point. They're not a revelation, more a reminder. These Rules are a starting point for you to pick up and run with.

I've tried to avoid the pedestrian (Time is a great healer) and the humorous (Never tip anyone who isn't looking) and the impractical (Love everyone), the plain daft (Turn the other cheek—you get hit twice that way, better to run I say), the wimpy (Everyone's a rainbow), the obviously wrong (There are no victims), and the very, very difficult (Spend 35 years in a cave, and you'll find the secret of the universe—and get a wet bottom). I've also avoided the trite (It'll be alright on the night—my experience is it never is) and the unpleasant (Don't get mad, get even).

I hope you, too, will follow a similar plan when you formulate new Rules for yourself. I guess the main thing is that you need to continually formulate your own Rules. When you learn something—from observation or just an illuminating moment—then absorb the lesson and see if there's a Rule there for future use.

# RULE 106

Try to find a new Rule every day—or at least occasionally. And I am quite genuine about wanting to know what you come up with—if you want to share them. Being a Rules Player is a lot of fun and quite fascinating to try and spot other Players. Whatever you do, though, don't go telling everyone about it. Keep it secret, keep it safe—but you can tell me: Richard.Templar@RichardTemplar.co.uk

Being a Rules Player requires dedication, hard work, perseverance, keenness, ambition, enthusiasm, devotion, and sheer doggedness. Keep at it, and you will live a fulfilled, happy, and productive life. But go easy on yourself; we all fail from time to time, and no one is perfect—I'm most certainly not. Enjoy, have fun, and be good.

THESE RULES ARE A
STARTING POINT FOR
YOU TO PICK UP AND
RUN WITH.